Peasant Entrepreneurship and Rural Poverty Reduction

The Case of Model Farmers in Bure Woreda, West Gojjam Zone

FSS Monograph No. 8

Abeje Berhanu and Ezana Amdework

𝔉𝔖𝔖

Forum for Social Studies (FSS)
Addis Ababa

ISBN: 978-99944-50-44-2

Layouts: Konjit Belete

Forum for Social Studies (FSS)
P.O. Box 25864 code 1000
Addis Ababa, Ethiopia
Email: fss@ethionet.et
Web: www.fssethiopia.org.et

This Monograph has been published with the financial support of the Norwegian Church Aid (NCA). The contents of the Monograph are the sole responsibilities of the author and can under no circumstances be regarded as reflecting the position of the NCA or the FSS.

Table of Contents

List of Tables

List of Plates

List of Acronyms

ACSI	Amhara Credit and Saving Institution
ADDP	Adaa District Development Project
AISCO	Agricultural Input Supply Corporation
ANRS	Amhara National Regional State
ANDM	Amhara National Democratic Movement
EPRDF	Ethiopian Peoples' Revolutionary Democratic Front
ARARI	Amhara Regional Agricultural Research Institute
ARDU	Arsi Rural Development Unit
BBM	Broad-Bed Maker)
BoARD	Bureau of Agricultural and Rural Development
CADU	Chillalo Agricultural Development Unit
CIS	Corrugated Iron Sheet
DA	Development Agent
DAP	Diammonium Phosphate
EC	Ethiopian Calendar
ECX	Ethiopian Commodity Exchange
EMTP	Extension Management Training Plot
FTC	Farmer Training Center
IPMS	Improving Productivity & Market Success
MALS	Meters Above Sea Level
MM	Millimeter
MPP	Minimum Package Project
NAEPP	New Agricultural Extension Package Program
PCs	Producers' Cooperatives
PADETS	Participatory Demonstration and Extension Training System
PASDEP	Plan for Accelerated and Sustained Development to End Poverty
SIDA	Swedish International Development Agency
SNNPR	Southern Nations, Nationalities and Peoples' Regional State
T &V	Technical and Vocational
USAID	United States Agency for International Development
WoARD	Wereda Office of Agriculture and Rural Development

Acknowledgments

The authors would like to acknowledge FSS for its financial and technical support, without which this research would not have been undertaken. We would also like to express our appreciation for the cooperation provided by the various offices of the Amhara National Regional State, including the regional BoARD, Cooperatives Promotion Agency, and Micro & Small Enterprise Development Agency; the Bure *woreda* Agriculture and Rural Development Office, and the Amhara Credit and Saving Institution (ACSI).

We would like to extend our thanks to the individuals who facilitated our work during primary data collection, namely Ato Dagnew Beza, Ato Getachew Addis, Ato Zemenu Tadesse, Ato Amanu Bitew, Ato Addisu Liku and W/t Habtam Niguse.

Finally, we are greatly indebted to our interviewees, including model farmers and non-model farmers, health extension workers, microfinance extension workers, agricultural extension workers and IPMS staff in Bure *woreda*.

About the Authors

Abeje Berhanu is currently an assistant professor of sociology, Department of Sociology, Addis Ababa University and Dean of Faculty of Social Sciences. He obtained his BA from Addis Ababa University (1987), MSC from the University of Arkansas, USA (1996) and PhD from the University of Queensland, Australia (2004). His research interests include farmers' adoption behavior of agricultural extension technologies, sociological dimension of agricultural extension, innovative practices of indigenous farming methods, farmer entrepreneurship, food security, community development, migration and rural development.

Ezana Amdework is a lecturer of sociology, Addis Ababa University and Assistant Dean of Faculty of Social Sciences. He earned his BA in Sociology and Social Anthropology in 2005 from the Department of Sociology and Social Anthropology, AAU (with great distinction and was awarded the university medal for outstanding students). He obtained his MA degree in Sociology from the same department in 2008. He has been involved in various research activities on urban and rural issues. His current research interests include rural-urban and international migration, industrial relations, urbanization, and the urban environment.

1. Introduction

1.1 Background

It is now a decade since Ethiopia started implementing a policy of poverty reduction and eradication. The government's poverty reduction and eradication program stresses the strategic importance of agriculture. The sector, however, is in the hands of millions of peasant producers who depend on traditional methods of cultivation of crops with limited use of green revolution technologies, such as chemical fertilizers. Ethiopia's ability to successfully break the vicious circle of famine and poverty is closely linked to improving the productivity of the smallholder agriculture that provides employment for more than 85% of the population and contributes to 43% of the GDP and 90% of the exports (MoARD, 2010). This requires effective use of both local and external farm inputs through the provision of integrated agricultural extension services.

The current package-based agricultural extension service, like its predecessors, uses 'model' farmers to disseminate improved technologies. This group of farmers, because of their entrepreneurial qualities, is expected to positively influence other farmers to adopt improved farming technologies. Farmer entrepreneurship occurs both within and outside agriculture. Within agriculture, it is manifested in the form of experimentation, and selection and adoption of innovative farming methods aimed at increasing farm productivity. Outside agriculture, peasant entrepreneurship occurs in the form of discovering and undertaking supplementary livelihood activities that are mainly located in the non-farm sector. Both efforts can contribute to rural poverty reduction.

This research focuses on the entrepreneurial experiences of 'model' farmers in the context of the current agricultural extension package program and their contribution to Ethiopia's poverty reduction efforts by taking the Bure Zuria *woreda* of the Amhara regional state as case study.

1.2 Problem Statement

To varying degrees and for different reasons, model farmers have always been part of agricultural development policies, programs and activities in Ethiopia. The Chillalo Agricultural Development Unit (CADU), which was launched in 1967, had as one of its components the involvement of model farmers in agricultural extension package demonstration and utilization (Berhanu, Hoekstra and Azage 2006: 15). Since then, model farmers have served as focal and entry points for rural development initiatives. The same is true with the most recent

1

Participatory Demonstration and Extension Training System (PADETS) approach.

More specifically, it is stated in the Government of Ethiopia's "Plan for Accelerated and Sustained Development to End Poverty (PASDEP)" policy document that farmer training centers (FTCs) are being used to strength agricultural extension services in the country. One of the major roles of the more than 5000 training centers is providing entrepreneurship skill development training to produce business-oriented farmers (MoFED 2006:88).

The aim of this research is, however, neither to investigate the nature of extension services in Ethiopia nor the problems and challenges they encounter. These issues have been extensively studied. Our primary concern here is to explore and gain an initial understanding of the phenomena of peasant entrepreneurship, which is believed to have contributed to the emergence of hundreds of "development heroes and heroines", some of whom are dubbed as "millionaire farmers".

Although there have always been farmer innovators/entrepreneurs, it is only recently that efforts to promote farmer entrepreneurship in a more organized manner is being undertaken by the federal and regional governments. This is evident in government organized annual farmers' festivals, which are aimed at acknowledging the endeavors and achievements of best performing farmers.

Therefore, it is high time that the factors that contribute to the entrepreneurial success of this group of farmers are studied and documented so that the insights to be gained will provide basis for future policy interventions.

1.3 Objectives

The general objective of this study is to assess the **immediate** (direct) and **contextual** (indirect) factors accounting for the entrepreneurial success of model farmers as well as their impact on other farmers with the ultimate goal of understanding the linkage between peasant entrepreneurship and rural poverty reduction.

More specifically, the study will investigate the following issues:

1. The immediate *personal, social, economic, and physical* factors that set apart "model farmers" from other farmers and thus account for their entrepreneurial success, including:

    a. Unique personal attributes of the household head (or principal manager of the farm and other livelihood activities) including upbringing, level of education and other personal experiences (such as previous involvement in off-farm employment, outside exposure, etc.);

b. Household features (household size, age and sex composition, health situation, educational level, and family members degree and nature of participation in productive work);

c. The presence and extent of utilization of social network and support systems (for example in the provision of seed money) and the benefits accrued thereof;

d. Degree of utilization of existing extension services (agricultural as well as small and microfinance extension), and access to financial capital;

e. Features of physical resources (including location vis-a-vis transportation arteries, water sources, fertility and size of land holding, etc.).

2. The contextual factors that allowed for greater farmer entrepreneurship, including *national and regional policies and programs*; as well as local level factors such as change in *community attitudes* towards innovation, adoption, entrepreneurship and personal success.

3. The processes through which these "model farmers" went, the significant steps they took (such as kinds of innovations they carried out, their engagement in off- and non-farm activities) and the challenges they faced in relation to their entrepreneurial activities.

4. Overall assessment of "model farmers" by other community members, mainly other ordinary farmers (including questions such as whether they are seen as change agents from whom others can learn or merely lucky or favored farmers);

5. Their impact on other farmers as well as the broader community. Have they positively influenced other farmers (has a spillover effect, that could positively contribute to the poverty reduction agenda, been created?).

1.4   Research Design and Methods

- *Study Design*

This study follows the case study design whereby Bure Zuria *Woreda* of the Amhara National Regional State is selected. Within the *woreda*[1] three *kebeles*[2], namely Weheni Durbete, Ziyew Shiwun, and Fetam Sentom were identified, each representing the three major agro-ecologies of *dega, woinadega*, and *qolla* respectively.[3] This enabled us investigate the distribution of peasant entrepreneurs across the different agro-ecologies as well as the nature of entrepreneurial activities carried out by peasants in the selected localities.

The selection of Bure Zuria as the case study *woreda* was based on the following criteria:

(1)   The *woreda* is characterized by agro-ecological diversity, namely it has all the major three agro-ecological zones – *dega, woinadega* and *qolla*.[4]

(2)   The relatively long experience of *woreda* with various agricultural extension programs; and

(3)   Presence of several accessible *kebeles* in the three agro-ecological zones of the *woreda*; and

(4)   The reported presence of a good number of model farmers in the *woreda*.

It is noteworthy that the employment of these selection criteria was crucial to the conduct of the study as the absence of anyone of them could have made the study difficult. Furthermore, the fact that the *woreda* has always been classified as a surplus producing *woreda* was another plus for the study. This and the above criteria taken together have created a situation under which the phenomenon of model farmers can be studied at its best.

1.5   Methods

The research has been carried out through the collection and analysis of primary and secondary data using intensive fieldwork conducted in the three *kebeles*. The

---

[1] Woreda (District), the third tier of government in Ethiopia's federal system of government. It is the level of government where much of services are provided.

[2] *Kebele* (country) the lowest level of local administration in Ethiopia

[3] The Amharic terms *dega, woinadega* and *qolla* refer respectively to highland, midland and lowland agro-ecology zones.

[4] Conventionally, Ethiopia is divided into three major agro-ecological zones, namely: *dega* (2300 – 3200 mals), *woinadega* (1500 – 2300), and *qolla* (500 – 1500).

fieldwork was undertaken in July and August of 2010 in two phases spanning a total of 18 days.

Primary data were collected using in-depth and key informant interviews and focus group discussions.

1. **In-depth interviews:** interviews were conducted with 16 model farmers from the three study *kebeles*. Even though the initial plan was to select 5 model farmers from each *kebele*, one additional model farmer was interviewed in Ziyew Shiwun, where the existence of diversified farming and non-farming activities was noted. The selection of interviewees was purposive with a view to obtaining as much in-depth information about the phenomenon of farmer entrepreneurship. As such, an attempt was made to include model farmers who have been awarded prizes at different farmers' festival.[5] Moreover, three female model farmers, one from each study *kebele* were interviewed.

   Qualitative data were mainly collected through this method in order to address two of the specific objectives stated above, namely the investigation of immediate factors that account for the entrepreneurial success of model farmers, and the assessment of the processes, steps and the challenges of farmer entrepreneurship. An interview guide containing semi-structured questions addressing the key issues of the study was administered.

2. **Key informant interviews** were conducted with agricultural development agents at the selected localities; *kebele* and *woreda* officials; *woreda* extension workers; small and micro-finance extension agents, as well as agriculture and rural development experts working in regional bureaus of agriculture and rural development. Issues raised here include extent of extension service utilization by model farmers, local and regional initiatives, and related strategies designed to encourage farmer entrepreneurship. Finally, knowledgeable community members have been interviewed to hear their views regarding farmer entrepreneurs in their localities. The selection of non-model farmers for interviews was made based on the recommendation given by *kebele* officials by taking into account our suggestion that certain members of the community such as priests, elders, and women, be included.

---

[5] Out of those interviewed, 1 got prize at the regional as well as national level in the year 2009/10, 2 were given prizes at zone level, and another 5 were recognized and given prizes at the *woreda* level.

3. **Focus group discussions (FGD)** with community members in the study localities were undertaken to generate data pertaining to the impact of "model farmers" on other farmers as well as the overall community views towards farmer entrepreneurship. The FGD is used to obtain information regarding community views towards peasant entrepreneurship in general. The FGDs were conducted using a guide/checklist containing major issues of discussion relevant to the topic under consideration. FGD participants were selected in a manner similar to the selection of non-model farmers – purposively.

In addition, secondary data relevant to the study was obtained and analyzed. The major sources of secondary data include:

- Reports of local governmental bodies and non-governmental organizations;
- Policy, program, and project documents;
- Published and unpublished research reports.

Using the above secondary sources, data have been collected regarding community features/characteristics, land use practices, extension input utilization, patterns of crop production and farm output and other related matters pertaining to each locality.

1.6   Scope

As indicated above, this study is informed wholly by data collected through qualitative techniques. This is done because of a number of reasons. First, in light of the relatively unstudied nature of the subject under investigation, this study opted to gain an initial understanding of the issue. Second, given the fewer distribution of model farmers among the farming population, it was necessary to employ a qualitative approach that specifically targeted a selected group of model farmers. It is our conviction that such an approach has enabled us to generate qualitative data that would help understand the experiences of selected model farmers and learn from their success stories.

However, care must be taken in trying to draw generalizations from the findings presented in the subsequent sections of the study as the data cannot be taken as representative of the study *woreda*, the region or the nation at large. More importantly, this research can be seen as a trailblazer for future research aimed at drawing general observations regarding the ways and means of replicating experiences in various parts of the country.

2. Model Farmer Approach in Ethiopian Extension Programs

2.1 The Imperial Era

In Ethiopia, government interest in agricultural extension service can be traced back to the establishment of the Ambo Agricultural School (1931). The School was the first in the country to offer instructions focusing on agriculture and related subjects. However, formal agricultural extension work began in the early 1950s following the establishment of the then Alemaya Agricultural College (1954), now Alemaya University. The main task of the College was to train agricultural professionals "in the higher technical and scientific branches of agriculture" (Pankhurst, 1957, quoted by Dessalegn, 2009: 33). Extension activities by the college began by employing two extension agents at Assela (Arsi) and Fitche (Shoa) and by establishing demonstrations centers for farmers.

Even though the College increased the number of extension agents, extension work was only concentrated in areas where the College had experimental stations which included Alemaya, Debre Zeit and Jimma. By 1963, 77 extension posts had been established with a total of 132 nationals serving in various areas. These agents were actively engaged in demonstration and helping farmers use new techniques in tools and machinery, insect and disease control and improved practices in the production of livestock and crops; paying regular visits to individual farmers; organizing and holding adult educational meetings and field days and encouraging the formation of agricultural youth clubs (Kassa, 2003).

However, it was during the Third Five-Year Development Plan (1968-73) that agricultural extension was given due consideration by the government. Unlike in the previous development plans (1957-68), where peasant agriculture was given little attention, it was during this time that the Imperial Government recognized the importance of smallholder peasant agriculture for the socio-economic development of the country. Consequently, an agricultural extension package approach designed to introduce the country to green revolution technologies was devised and implemented in few selected areas of the country.

Cognizant of the country's limited resources to simultaneously modernize peasant agriculture across the country, the government opted for the comprehensive package approach. This involved the coordinated application of different but related strategies, such as improving the existing infrastructure, dispensing better and well organized social services and providing effective transportation, marketing and credit services as well as popularizing appropriate, well-tested and locally-adapted improved agricultural technologies. The rationale here was that progress made in selected sites would have multiplier effects on the surrounding areas by way of demonstration and as a result of social interaction.

The first comprehensive package project, the Chillalo Agricultural Development Unit (CADU), was established as an autonomous entity in the Arsi region. Based on the experience gained from CADU, whose extension activities in turn were modeled on the experience of Comilla multi-purpose project in the then East Pakistan (now Bangladesh) (Dessalegn, 2009), other autonomous comprehensive package projects with varying objectives and approaches were initiated. These included the Wolaita Agricultural Development Unit; the Adaa District Development Project; the Tach Adiabo and Hedekti Agricultural Development Unit in the northwest of Tigray; the Southern Region Agricultural Development Project in the vicinity of Hadassah town; and the Humera Agricultural Development (Cohen, 1987; Kassa, 2003). The main aim of these projects was to disseminate improved farming practices among farmers through the use of chemical fertilizers, improved seeds and market access to smallholders.

However, not all farmers in the project areas responded to the newly introduced farming technologies in the same manner. As expected, some were more receptive than others in perceiving the benefits of adopting improved farming practices. Such group of farmers was given the name 'model farmer' and were used to influence fellow farmers to adopt new farming practices. Development agents were assigned to assist model farmers with the task of implementing recommended technology packages. Here, model farmers' plots were used to demonstrate the application of new farming innovations (Fasil, 1993), from which other farmers were expected to learn good farming practices. Tesfai (1977: 289) defined the model farmer approach as follows:

> The 'model'-farmer approach is a strategy in which extension agents work closely with one selected farmer per area of about 100 farmers, at the same time running their own demonstration plots, which are strategically placed near major roads, market places, or churches. The aim was to 'provide each selected 'model farmer' with needed training and supervision regarding the use of new agricultural practices, hoping that neighboring farmers will be favorably influenced by his success and will wish to adopt the new practices.

CADU and ADDP used the model farmer approach throughout the project areas to scale up their extension activities. As noted by Cohen (1987), the use of the model farmer approach was one of the building blocks of the CADU extension approach. Cohen described the process of identifying and selecting model farmers by CADU as follows. First, project staff would call a gathering of farmers living within an 800 ha designated area (this would be equivalent to the size of *Kebele* boundaries under the Derg[6]). Second, the staff would give a briefing to the gathering regarding the objectives and aims of the project and associated benefits of participation in the project. Third, the participants would be asked to select a committee of five people, among whom one would be selected as a model farmer by the project staff. To be selected as a model farmer, one was expected to meet the following criteria (Cohen, 1987):

- Farming should be a full-time occupation

- Should be a resident in the community

- Should hold plots suitable and accessible to demonstrations

- Should be willing to assign plots as demonstration sites

- Should be a person of good moral character

There were some 414 model farmers covering 42,000 farm households residing in the CADU project area by the end of 1973. This means on average there were up to 100 farmers under every model farmer. Extension agents were closely working with model farmers, who would in turn work with fellow farmers in their respective villages.

CADU's review of the model farmer approach resulted in positive assessments noting that model farmers were *imminently suitable information disseminators ... a relatively cheap method for reaching the grassroots level* (Quoted by Cohen, 1987: 85). The majority of model farmers shared their newly acquired knowledge with other farmers in their areas. It also became apparent that some of the model farmers selected in 1968 had expanded their holdings by as much as three times ceasing to be average farmers in their areas in 1970 (Bergman, 1970 cited in Cohen, 1987).

As Cohen pointed out, there were, however, suggestions by development agents that CADU should broaden its extension base by focusing on a more inclusive group of innovative farmers that could bring collective impact on a given area. CADU's approach was also criticized for being pro-rich farmers, with landlords reaping almost all the extension services provided by CADU project staff. WADU from the beginning did not use this strategy saying it would favor certain section of the farming population that had the resources and connections to take advantage of the new farming technologies.

---

[6] Amharic/Geez word for a committee – it refers to the military government that ruled Ethiopia from 1974-1991.

2.2 The Derg Period

Agricultural extension services during the mid-1970s through the 1980s focused on farmer-to-farmer extension delivery method. However, this was not done vigorously and consistently because of shortage of resources and the necessity of covering wider geographical areas with limited extension staff. Here, mention can be made of the Minimum Package Project I (MPP I), Minimum Package Project II (MPP II) and the Peasant Agricultural Development and Extension Project (PADEP) of the 1970s and 1980s. The main goal, with varying degree of emphasis between the projects, was to reach a large number of farmers by making use of the technologies generated and tested by the comprehensive package projects. Both contact farmers and extension agents were encouraged to demonstrate the importance of improved techniques of production to other farmers.

Here, too, it would appear easier for DAs to work under the assumption that if they could influence a group of motivated and innovative farmers, others would gradually adopt farming methods used by progressive farmers. For example, under PADEP, extension agents had to work with a group of contact farmers that received regular visits of four days a week and each contact farmer had 26 follower farmers (Kassa, 2003).

Generally, under the Derg, the model farmer extension approach was subdued in favor of producers' cooperatives and collective farms at the expense of smallholder individual farmers. Besides, development agents (DAs) were burdened with non-extension activities such as carrying out party propaganda that tarnished their credibility among peasants. In 1981, DAs altogether ceased working with smallholder farmers. Service and producer cooperatives (PCs) became focal points for introducing extension innovations. Moreover, producers' cooperatives continued to enjoy preferential treatment in terms of access to formal credit and modern agricultural technologies.

As compared to smallholders, PCs used to pay 10% less for 100kg of fertilizers and less tax per hectare. Thus the rate of technological adoption on farms owned and operated by PCs was relatively higher than individual smallholders. For instance, in the Bako area of western Ethiopia all PCs farms used fertilizers and improved maize varieties, while only 34% and 50% of smallholders used improved maize varieties and fertilizers respectively (Legesse & Asfaw, 1988, cited by Gizachew, 2008).

Even if the idea of model farmer is associated with individual households, as the Derg was interested to expand cooperatives, the focus was on model cooperatives rather than model farmers.

2.3   The Recent Experience

The use of the model farmer approach by the Ethiopian extension system with its variant of contact-farmer approach continued after the fall of the Derg. In this respect, in the early 1990s the Transitional Government of Ethiopia adopted the World Bank-initiated Training and Visit (T&V) extension system. This system was characterized, among others, by regular extension-farmer contact and training as major pillars for the organization and delivery of extension services. Once again, farmer-to-farmer extension through contact farmers was used as the main strategy for the dissemination and delivery of messages and technology packages. Similarly, the Sasakawa Global-2000 project which emphasized on green technologies also used the T & V approach.

Based on the experiences of the Sasakawa-Global 2000   that was pilot-tested in selected areas of the SNNPR, Oromiya and Amhara regions in 1993/94-1994/95, a comprehensive national extension system was launched in 1995. The introduction of the participatory demonstration and extension training system (PADETS), otherwise known as the new agricultural extension package program (NAEPP), was marked by its use of 'model farms' as a focal point in the dissemination of improved technologies. Such farms, given the name 'extension management training plots' (EMTP) were owned and managed by the participating farmers with extension workers regularly visiting and supervising the implementation of technology packages as per the recommendations given by *woreda*/zone-level agriculture and extension offices. As noted by Kassa (2003), extension agents used the EMTPs to train both participating and neighboring farmers so that they can put into practice packages of recommended practices. The farmers running the EMTPs were seen as models not only by the extension staff but also by neighboring farmers against whom they compared yields of plots cultivated with and without recommended extension packages.

As the name implies, the philosophy of PADETS has become (1) participatory extension service (2) through the establishment of half-hectare demonstration plots that are (3) owned and managed by the farmers themselves, and (4) with the DA expected to provide on-site training and supervision for the farmer. Participation in the extension package program was equated to establishing EMTPs. EMPTs were established in all parts of the country and running an EMPT became the rule rather than the exception of the new extension package program.

In 1995/96, the Ethiopian government sponsored the establishment of about 36,000 on-farm demonstrations. In the 1996/97, 1997/98 and 1998/99 production years, the number of government-sponsored demonstration plots was 600,000, 2.9 million and 3.8 million, respectively (Kassa, 2003). The trend is for this number to keep growing. Likewise, the number of farmers participating in the new extension program increased from 35,000 in 1995- 1996 to 3.7 million in 1998-1999.

By early 2000s, EMTPs became PADETS's widely used implementing tools. Possession of half hectare of land and willingness to allocate the plot for on-farm demonstration became a requirement for participation in the extension program. A farmer who had agreed to implement EMTPs was required to (1) follow DA recommendation in the application of extension packages – chemical fertilizers and seeds, (2) make the plot open for DA supervision and (3) make the farm accessible to fellow farmers to visit and copy 'best' extension practices. The government in return gave such farmers access to farm credit to buy chemical fertilizers and improved seeds.

Soon DAs became busy persuading farmers to establish EMTPs as their performance evaluation mostly depended on the number of EMTPs within the DA's area of operation. EMTPs became the centerpiece of the interaction among extension agents, participating farmers and non-participating farmers who might be searching for inspiration from innovative/early adoptive farmers. Hence, the model farm approach has been at the center in the implementation of the extension package program.

With the deepening of the activities of PADETS into the 2000s, the model farm approach that focuses on extension-managed plot has been transformed into the individual model farmer approach. Here, attention shifted from 'plot' as a farm model to the 'farmer' as a model for fellow farmers, as an entrepreneur. When the 'plot' is taken as a farm model, the single most important evaluative criterion is the ability of the farmer to successfully apply recommended technology packages on a single farm; whereas when a farmer is taken as a 'model', his/her achievements are assessed against a multiple set of criteria that include not only success in farming but also outside farming. This leads us to the current understanding of the concept of 'model farmer', which is much broader and comprehensive touching almost every aspect of the farmer and his/her family.

2.4   Current Use of the Concept Model Farmer

Currently, a model farmer is one who has a proven record of success in his/her farming as well as non-farming endeavors. Success in farming, which is a major indicator of being a model farmer, is measured in terms of (1) successful adoption of extension package technologies according to the instructions given by the DA (for instance, correct application of fertilizers and seeds, preparation of compost, etc.), (2) increased productivity in the production of major cereals, and (3) production of market-oriented crops, such as red pepper, sesame, and improved maize seed. Success in non-farming activities entails undertaking a wide range of off-farm income generating activities, such as small trade, renting a house, running a horse/mule cart and establishing a warehouse in town. Besides, a model farmer is expected to be a leader/model in his community by sending all school-age children to school, by keeping his house in order (e.g. respecting family members and involving them in decision-making), by actively participating in community affairs (e.g. being a good *shimagle*[7]), and by implementing the health extension package which has 12 components.

Taking the above criteria into consideration, the designation of a farmer as a 'model farmer' is decided by the *kebele* leadership that consists of *kebele* administrator, deputy administrator, coordinator of the *kebele* agricultural development station, head of security in the area, representatives of women and youth organizations, the health extension worker, and the school director. In doing so, they use a set of criteria which include, in addition to those listed above, active participation in natural resource management (e.g. soil conservation and forestation), acceptance by the community and ability to influence others. Similar criteria are more or less used across the study *kebeles*.

In connection with this, it is important to indicate the sometimes overlapping use of terminologies on the ground. In all of the study *kebeles* there was a distinct group of farmers who are identified as 'model' on the basis of the afore-mentioned criteria. The purpose of selection of this pool of farmers relates to the establishment of the extension packages users group, commonly known as the 'development team', the leaders of which have to be exemplary farmers who can serve as models for others. Model farmers are those who are primarily in the fore-front in the adoption of farming innovations. They are targets in the dissemination of agricultural technologies, such as chemical fertilizers and seeds.[8]

The other commonly used term, namely "*ginbar kedem*' was originally used to refer to some 300 farmers selected in each *kebele* and trained by the ruling party. While some of these are indeed model farmers in the sense used above, a few others were not farmers let alone model farmers. However, the term '*ginbar kedem'* is being used in some cases synonymously with model farmer. For instance, in the two study *kebeles*, namely Ziyew Shiwun and Fetam Sentom, the two terms were used interchangeably to refer to farmers who are successful in their farming as well as non-farming endeavors. In these two *kebeles*, farmers

---

[7]Respected elder who serves as an arbitrator in dispute/conflict resolution.

[8]Mamusha & Hoffman (2005) reported that some model farmers in Debre Birhan were selected on the basis of their relationship to local leadership and political patronage. Also a study by Gizachew (2008) found that model farmers were largely selected by the DA. However, the present study could not substantiate these two claims.

who are party members are referred to simply as *"ye dirijit abal"*, meaning member of ANDM/EPRDF.

In Weheni Durbete *kebele*, the term model farmer and *'ginbar kedem'* were, however, used distinctly with the second referring to farmers who were members of the ruling party.

The study has also come across another use of the term model farmer, where it is used for someone who is exceptionally successful in one particular agricultural or non-agricultural task. Accordingly, one might be recognized as a model farmer in the production of compost, or construction of terracing, and the like. Also present is the categorization of farmers into **A, B** and **C**, which was still being undertaken during the field work for the study. The criteria used to select level '**A**' farmers are almost the same as those used to select model farmers in the study *kebele* (see **Annex I** for a complete list of the criteria).

Perhaps the clearest criteria and selection procedure are the ones set for the selection of farmers for awards at the annual farmers' festivals. The guideline for the selection of awardees for Fourth Farmers' Festival, for instance, stipulates that there will be a awards in four categories: those who have added value, new awardees, youth and women. According to the guideline, a committee comprised of the *kebele* chairman, manager and DA, two respected elders and representatives of *kebele* youth and women organizations will recommend awardees on the basis of the set criteria to the *woreda* Farmers' Festival Organizing Committee. This committee in turn will reach a decision regarding the candidates and send the names to the regional relevant committee (see *Annex II* for the complete selection criteria).

To sum up, in the context of the delivery and management of current agricultural extension services in Ethiopia, the concept of 'model farmer' is applied more broadly to include innovative farmer attributes that occur both within and outside agricultural extension. A model farmer is not only expected to exhibit exemplary farm practices (e.g. proper management of soils, correct application of chemical fertilizers and seeds) but also engage in activities which are considered innovative and new in the area. Therefore, it really makes sense to talk about the model farmer as an innovator, as an entrepreneur.

2.5   Model Farmer as an Entrepreneur

In the past, the use of model farmer as an extension information dissemination strategy was limited to activities related to adoption of agricultural extension packages as per the recommendation given by the extension agent. Here, a model farmer would be one who partially or wholly adheres to the extension agent's advice regarding the application of the right amount of DAP and urea to a certain hectare of land or the adoption of a high-yielding variety corn seed. This is similar to Ryan and Gross's classic diffusion study where innovative farmers were among the five adopter categories who were the first to adopt the hybrid corn seed that was released in Iowa in 1928 (Rogers, 1983).

In many respects, today's model farmers are entrepreneurs, and as such expected to be pioneers not only in farm activities but also in off-farm income generating activities such as town-based small businesses, for example, running a coffee/tea shop. Model farmers are leaders in the adoption of new farming technologies and are considered role models for other farmers to follow. They are expected to demonstrate their leadership skills in farming by being at the fore-front of the experimentation of improved corn seeds, correct application of fertilizer and seed packages, preparation of organic fertilizers/compost, undertaking soil conservation practices (e.g. terracing) and in the application of zero-tillage. They are also leaders in their communities as *shimaglis* in conflict resolution,

However, it should be noted that the concept of model farmer is a relative term and differs from place to place. For example, a model farmer in *woinadega* areas has a wide range of engagements and undertakings usually combining farm and non-farm activities. On the other hand, the innovativeness of those in the *dega* is limited to a few areas of activities (e.g. they cultivate limited number of crops) due to ecological risks/limitations thereby offering limited opportunities for expansion of both farm and non-farm activities. One can appreciate the adverse impact of the physical environment in the *dega* (land, soil and conditions) on farmers' innovativeness by looking at the limited number of crops that grow there and the depletion of ecological resources. It is not by coincidence that the number of model farmers increases as altitude decreases (see 3.4). Current ecological resources (e.g. availability of land, diversity of crops, etc) are conducive for engagement by farmers in entrepreneurial activities in the *woinadega-qolla* areas.

2.6   Conceptual Framework

The view that small farmers engage in entrepreneurial activities of both farm and non-farm nature designed to improve their welfare and the welfare of their family members is no longer debatable. Scholars and practitioners who have maintained longstanding interest in the condition of the rural people in developing countries observed that farmers, especially resource-poor farmers, continuously experiment, adapt and innovate (Chambers *et al.*, 1989).

In his seminal work on rural development (1983), Chambers noted that farmers maintain an experimental mentality in their interaction with the land and crops. He specifically cited the case of seed selection by farmers involving trial and error drawing upon centuries of accumulated rural people's knowledge and expertise. In his book on *'Indigenous Agricultural Revolution'*, Richards (1985) also presented a wealth of empirical evidence of the inventive capacity of small-scale farmers. This has been confirmed by several studies including that of Nielsen (2001, quoted by Wu, 2003) who identified 1614 innovative practices carried out by 505 East African farmers.

Kibwana *et al.* (2001) documented the experience of local farmer innovators in experimenting with improved land husbandry practices in Tigray. In order to assist local innovations, Mekele University established a database of farmer innovators and by early 2000s as many as 100 entries were made. It is noted that many of these farmers have innovated in multiple ways on a single farm, including but not limited to undertaking informal experiments, such as using a donkey-plough rather than sticking to the conventional oxen-plough. Here an innovator is defined as *someone who develops new ideas without support from formal research and extension* (Kibwana et al., 2001: 134). Local innovators are farm managers and leaders who make decisions that carry risks and hence display the characteristic features of an entrepreneur. Peasant entrepreneurs like any other group of entrepreneurs are characterized by innovativeness and vision. In addition, they manifest optimistic, self-confident and risk-taking behaviors and are willing to experiment and try new ways of doing things, such as complementing their farm income with non-farm incomes. Also, they possess certain skill sets that are not available in the wider farm population.

Lichtenstein and Lyons (2001; cited in Smith, Schallenkamp & Douglas, 2007) identified a set of skills required for the success of entrepreneurs. These skills are defined in four major categories; namely (1) technical skills, (2) managerial skills, 3) entrepreneurial skills, and 4) personal maturity and social responsibility skills. Following this, in our study of **peasant entrepreneurship** (Figure 1), technical skills consist of three sub-sets: (1) level of comprehension of technical information, including ability to write and read, (2) ability to make the necessary farm provisions at the right time and in the right place, including purchase of extension inputs, and (3) ability to acquire the necessary farm tools, maintain and update them when necessary. The managerial skills category comprises of four sub-sets, namely (1) management – planning, organizing, supervising, directing, networking, (2) financial – bookkeeping, cost/benefit analysis, (3) market – recognition of marketable products, searching buyers/customers, storing for better prices, and (4) administrative/ legal – managing relations between people and local administration.

Figure 1: Conceptual framework showing peasant entrepreneurial skills, adapted from Lichtenstein & Lyons (2001)

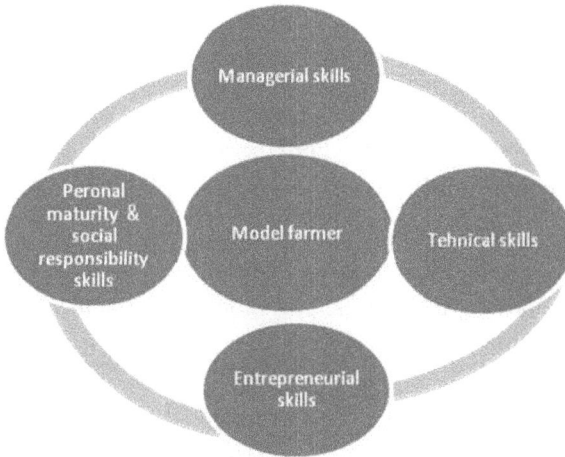

SOURCE: Authors

Model farmers' entrepreneurial skills include four sub-components (1) business concept – business plan, (2) ability to sense and capture market opportunities, (3) technology adoption – pioneering in the adoption of technologies promoted by the extension service, and (4) risk-taking behavior. Finally, the personal maturity and social responsibility skill set consists of four sub-sets, namely (1) self-awareness/confidence - ability to reflect and be introspective, (2) accountability – ability to take responsibility for resolving a problem, (3) social responsibility – ability to take leadership role in the community, and (4) being a model farmer – ability and willingness to positively influence fellow farmers so that they can improve their situations.

The four categories of entrepreneurial skills and the different sub-sets described in Figure 1 together form peasant entrepreneurial skill sets. The conceptual framework provides a heuristic device for analyzing and assessing entrepreneurial experiences of model farmers in terms of the skills discussed here. This task is undertaken in sections 4.1 through 4.3. A central proposition of this study is that most model farmers in the study area exhibit an array of entrepreneurial skills that are possessed by a very limited number of the farming community in each locality/ *kebele* and those with these skills are rated by their neighbors as successful farmers – model farmers.

Of course model farmers as entrepreneurs do not function in a vacuum – their success depends on a combination of micro-level (individual and household characteristics) and macro-level (policy environment) factors. The first set of attributes are related to personal characteristics of individual model farmers and their level of access to what development experts call 'capital assets', including human capital, social capital, financial capital, physical and environmental/ecological capital. The question now is whether model farmers had a privileged position initially (resulting from a combination of family background, political or social circumstances) with respect to these assets or whether they have improved their level of access to the assets over the years. The second attribute (i.e. policy dimension) concerns the impact of government policy (e.g. agricultural and rural development policy) on the activities of model farmers and whether the extension program and other supporting services are biased towards model farmers in the provision of developmental services to the farming communities.

3. Description of the Study Setting

3.1 Location and Population

The Amhara National Regional State (ANRS) is one of the nine regional states of the Federal Democratic Republic of Ethiopia. Geographically, ANRS lies between 9^0-14^0 N and 36^0-40^0E and covers an area of some 170,752 km^2. In terms of land size, it is the third largest region after Oromiya and Somali regions and the 2nd most populous (after Oromiya) with over 17 million inhabitants. The ANRS is located in the northwestern and north-central parts of the country and is bordered by Tigray in the north, Afar in the east, Benishangul-Gumuz in the west and Oromiya in the south. It shares an international boundary with the Republic of the Sudan in the west.

Average population density in the region is 100 persons per km^2 and ranges from 236 persons per km^2 in Tehuledere *Woreda* in north Wollo to 5 persons per km^2 in Quara *Woreda* in north Gondar. The region is sub-divided into 10 zones and one special zone (Awi zone), 105 *woreda* and 3,105 rural *kebeles*. As it is an ethnically organized state like the rest of Ethiopia, more than 90% of the people in the region are Amhara from which the region's name is derived.

3.2 Land and Economy

Land plays a critical role in the economy of the region where smallholder agriculture predominates. It is estimated that during a given planting season about 52% of the total land of the region would be cultivated. Forest cover represents a meager 1% of the region's land and there is some regeneration of bush land, woodland, shrubs and grassland due to recent enclosure and planting activities by governmental bodies, communities and individual households. Ancient human habitation and century-old farming practices have contributed to deforestation.

Because of high population pressure, average plot holding is less than 1 ha per farm household. Several rounds of land redistribution during the military regime and major land redistribution undertaken by the EPRDF-led Amhara regional government in 1997 resulted in fragmentation of plots. Consequently as succinctly put by Dessalegn (2009: 139), *each generation of peasants [in the Amhara region] inherits land which is smaller than before.* Landlessness is particularly acute among young people who in some areas are being forced to cultivate marginal plots whenever available or rent land from older and female-headed households at very expensive rates.

Crop cultivation together with livestock herding provide for 90% of the livelihood of the people in the region. For instance, cereal production accounts for 82 % of the cultivated land in *meher*[9] 2010. Main crops include teff, barely, wheat, maize, sorghum and finger millet. Pulses and oilseeds, which have become important sources of cash for rural households, are also widely grown in the *woinadega/dega* and in the *qolla* areas respectively. The oxen-drawn plough is the principal means of land traction, though hoe-farming is also practiced by *qolla* farmers that cultivate steep soils. Owing to the steep nature of the plots (slope gradient ranges from 5^0-45^0) and lack of improved land management practices land degradation, de-vegetation and soil erosion (annual soil loss in overgrazed and steep lands reaches 300 tons/ha) are serious problems affecting the subsistence base of the population.

3.3 Agricultural Zones

According to the BoARD, the region is divided into two major agricultural zones, western and eastern Amhara. The former consists of five zones, namely East Gojjam, Awi, West Gojjam, South Gondar and North Gondar. The latter comprises North Wollo, South Wollo, North Shewa, Waghimera and Oromiya zones. While western Amhara is mono-cropping and solely dependent on *meher* rains for the cultivation of crops, eastern Amhara is characterized by a bi-modal rainfall – *belg*[10] rains from January through March and *meher* rains from May to September with high intensity in June through August. From the point of view of utilization of extension services, western Amhara is a high extension input-user region, according to officials of the BoARD.

The Amhara Regional Agricultural Research Institute (ARARI) which was established in 2000 is responsible for undertaking agricultural research and extension activities in the region. ARARI operates eight research centers, namely Adet, Sirinka, Debre Birhan, Sekota, and Gondar Research Centers, Bahir Dar Fishery and Agricultural Mechanization Research Center and Andassa Livestock Research Center and five sub-centers, at Finote Selam, Debre Tabor, Kobo, Hayk and Addis Ketema.

3.4 The Study *Woreda*

3.4.1 Location and Physical Features of Bure Woreda

Bure *Woreda*[11], which is located in West Gojjam zone, provides the immediate study site for this research. The *woreda* was selected for this study because of its

---

[9]Refers to main rainy season from June through August which is the main growing season in Ethiopia.
[10]Refers to small rains season from January through March.
[11]Although our study focuses on Bure Zuria *Woreda*, the description provided hereunder includes the Bure Town Administration, which has 8 *kebeles* as well. As far as Bure Zuria *Woreda* is concerned, it has 19 rural *kebele* and a population of 120,565 persons (male 60659, female 59906).

long experience in the use of extension inputs going back to the imperial period, current high usage of extension inputs (e.g. chemical fertilizers and seeds), relatively diversified agricultural activities and accessibility to transportation.

Bure is one of the 15 *woreda* found in southeast part of the west the Gojjam zone. It shares borders with the following *woreda* of the region – Finote Selam in the east, Webberima and Shindi in the west; Akum in the north and Bacquna in the northwest and the East Wellega zone of the Oromiya regional state in the south. The *Woreda* with its capital at Bure town located 400 km from Addis Ababa and 148 km from Bahir Dar consists of 19 rural *kebeles*.

Plate 1: Map of Bure *Woreda* and the *Kebeles*

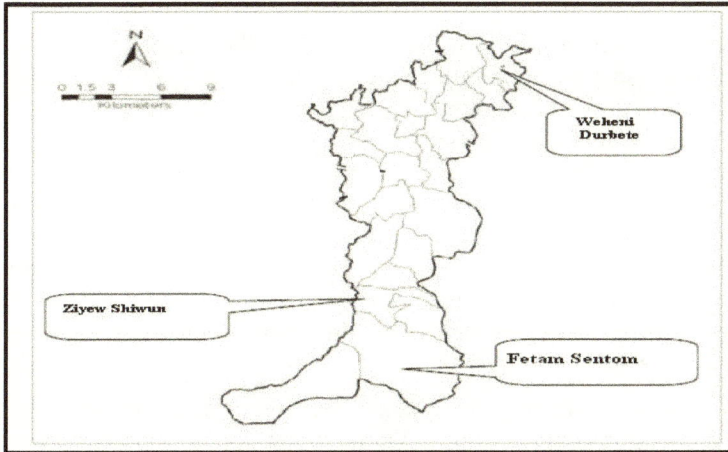

The *Woreda* has an estimated population of about 170,000 people (1% of the region's population) that reside in an estimated 24,579 households (Table 1). Some 12% of the households are female-headed and this figure might be on the rise as women are now receiving land title deeds in their names. As can be seen in Table 1 below, the proportion of females is slightly higher than that of males.

21

Table 1: Population and Number of Households by Sex in Rural and Urban Areas of Bure *Woreda*

Location	Total Population			Number of Households		
	Male	Female	Total	Male	Female	Total
Rural	72033	71821	143854	19226	2567	21793
Urban	11633	13122	25755	1699	1087	2786
Total	83666	85943	169609	20925	3654	24579

SOURCE: Bure Pilot Learning *Woreda* Diagnosis and Program Design, July 2007

The *Woreda* is predominantly *woinadega* (82%), though *qolla* and *dega* agro-ecologies are also present. Altitude ranges from 713 masl in the south near the Abbay gorge to 2604 masl around Wehine Dur Bete *Kebele* in the north. Bure *Woreda* receives relatively high amount of rainfall ranging from 1386 mm to 1757 mm annually. Being characterized by a mono-modal agro-ecology, rainfall occurs from June through August but also May and September may enjoy good rains as was the case in 2010. As expected, annual temperatures drop with rising elevations with most of the *Woreda* experiencing an average temperature of 17 to 18 degree Celsius. An abundance of good rainfall, favorable temperature and relatively fertile *woinadega* and *qolla* plots make Bure one of the surplus-producing *woredas* in the region.

Like the rest of Ethiopia in general and the region in particular, 85% of the population lives in rural areas in 21,793 farm households. This gives an average household size of 6 members. Population density is 233 persons per km^2, total area of the *Woreda* being 727.4 km^2.

3.4.2 *Land Use Patterns and Farming Systems*

Land provides a lifeline for almost every farm household in the *Woreda*. It is not only a source of food but also a source of domestic energy in the form of wood, crop residues and cow dung. Although land is used for multiple purposes (including but not limited to animal pasture, forestry, construction) cultivation of crops constitutes a major land use type in the *Woreda*. Major cultivated crops include teff, maize, wheat and finger millet. Root crops such as potato (*woinadega* and *dega* areas) and fruits such as papaya, avocado and orange (*woinadega* and *qolla* areas) are also widely cultivated.

Accordingly, 47% of the *Woreda's* land is devoted to crop production during the 2010 *meher* season. The rest of the land is covered by forest, bush, shrubs and grasses. Natural and manmade forests cover 6143 and 401 ha of land respectively. There is a noticeable coverage of eucalyptus tree (mostly grown in dedicated plots but also around homesteads and farms as fences), which has become an important source of cash for farm households mainly in the *woinadega* and *dega* areas.

According to the Bure Pilot Learning Diagnosis and Program Design study, the *Woreda* has two major farming systems. These include cereal/pepper/livestock complex and cereal/potato/ livestock complex. The first farming system appears to be more prevalent in the *woinadega* and *qolla* areas, while the second is common in the *dega* and *woinadega* localities. Two other additional farming systems can be also identified – cereal/oilseeds/livestock and cereal/fruits/ livestock complex, which are practiced in the *dega/woinadega* and *woinadega/ qolla* agro-ecologies respectively.

3.5 The Study *Kebeles*

As has been stated in the methodology section, this qualitatively-oriented study focuses on three *kebeles* within the Bure *Woreda* – Weheni Durbete, Ziyew Shiwun and Fetam Sentom – as case studies. Each of the three study *kebele* represents *dega*, *woinadega* and *qolla* agro-ecologies respectively. The elevations and patterns of distribution of average annual rainfall and temperature in the three study *kebeles* are shown in Table 2 below.

Table 2: Study *Kebeles* by Altitude, Amount of Rainfall, Temperature and Agro-ecology

Kebele	Altitude (meters)	Rainfall (mm)	Temperature (^{0}C)	Agro-ecology
Weheni Durbete	1879-2604	1604-1659	14-16	*Dega*
Ziyew Shiwun	1879-2166	1544-1659	17-18	*Woinadega*
Fetam Sentom	773-1231	1386-1659	21-24	*Qolla*

SOURCE: Bure Pilot Learning *Woreda* Diagnosis and Program Design, July 2007.

As can be seen in Table 3, population density is highest in *dega* - twice the *woinadega* and four times the *qolla kebele*. This has implication for the availability of agricultural land and also local innovations. In the Weheni Durbete where there is scarcity of land, the level and diversity of local innovations resulting in part from the adoption of technology packages by farmers appears to be limited. Accordingly, the distribution of the number of model farmers tends to vary by agro-ecology zone.

Table 3: Household Size, Population, and Area of the Three Study *Kebeles*

Kebele	Household size			Population			Area Km²
	Male	Female	Total	Male	Female	Total	
Weheni Durbete	1119	145	1264	4035	4275	8310	17.2
Ziyew Shiwun	1176	153	1329	3667	4008	7675	37.1
Fetam Sentom	1052	136	1188	3934	3713	7647	79.6

SOURCE: Bure Pilot Learning *Woreda* Diagnosis and Program Design, July 2007

The study used data obtained from focus group discussions conducted among community members to assess economic status of residents in each of the study *kebele* and solicited rough estimates of the percentage of *kebele* residents falling in the categories of poor, middle and rich. The results are presented in Table 4.

Table 4: Percentages of Residents Falling in Different Wealth Categories by Study *Kebele*

Wealth Category	Study *Kebele*		
	Weheni Durbete	Ziyew Shiwun	Fetam Sentom
Rich	Owns a house in town, or owns flour mill, or has residential house with corrugated iron sheet (CIS) roof, 2 pairs of oxen, 3 milk cows *(10%*)*	Engages in wholesale grain trade, 2 or more CIS houses in town, has one or more mule drawn carts *(5%)*	Engages in wholesale grain trade, 3 pairs of oxen, two or more CIS houses in town, has stores or shops rented in town *(30%)*
Middle	Residential house with CIS roof, a pair of oxen, 2 milk cows *(60%)*	Rents small shop, or cafeteria, or has one or more carts, produces enough for food and market *(85%)*	Owns 2 or more oxen, engaged in the production of cash crops (e.g. sesame), CIS house *(65%)*
Poor	Straw-roofed house, 1 or no ox, 1 or no milk cow *(30%)*	No side business, 1 or no ox, 50 CIS or less house *(10%)*	Straw-roofed house, owns only one ox *(5%)*

* Percentage of population in the locality falling in that particular wealth category.

As can be seen in Table 4, although there are variations among the three *kebeles*, some common denominators appear. This is especially true of the category of "rich", where ownership of a house in town is a key indicator, along with one or more non-farm business activities, such as running a flour mill. However, the two *kebeles*, namely Ziyew Shiwun and Fetam Sentom, appear to have more things in common as relating to undertaking wholesale trade, which is an indicative of farmers' engagement in commercial activities.[12]

In this section, a brief description of each study *kebele* will follow. The information used here is obtained from development agents (DAs) working in the respective *kebele*, from *kebele* managers responsible for the day-to-day operation of the *kebele* administration and from staff working in the Bure *Woreda* Office of Agriculture and Rural Development (WOARD).

3.5.1 Weheni Durbete Kebele

Weheni Durbete *Kebele* is located in the northeast part of the *Woreda* at a distance of 18 km from Bure town, 6 km off the right-hand turn at Mankussa town of the main Addis Ababa-Bahir Dar road. The *Kebele* is named by combining three sub- *kebeles – gote[13]* namely Weheni, Durbete and Sube. It has common borders with two *woredas* – Finote Selam and Akum in the east and north respectively– and with two adjacent *kebeles* – Agem Fereda and Arbisi Menfesawit in the west and south respectively.

The *Kebele* covers an area of 17.2 km² and is inhabited by 8310 persons in 1264 households (female-headed households account for 11.5%). Population density is about 489 persons per km². This puts Weheni Durbete as the second (after *woinadega* Wangedam *kebele* with a population of 10971 and an area of 19 km²) most densely populated *kebele* in the *Woreda*. Consequently, average landholding is 0.75 ha with plot size varying from 0.25 to 1.5 ha. The acute shortage of land is evident in the fact that 89.3% of the farmland has been covered by crops during the 2010 *meher* season. One can appreciate the seriousness of the land shortage issue in the *Kebele* by noting that most households are forced to graze their cows and oxen around the borders of their croplands and farmsteads.

Cereal production constitutes a major land use system in the *Kebele* (Table 5). For instance, the major crops cultivated during the 2010 *meher* season in order of the size of plots include maize, finger millet, teff, barley, wheat and some

---

[12] For the socio-economic profile of interviewed informants, model as well as non-model, see *Annex III*.

[13] A geographical area inhabited by farm households belonging to the same neighborhood.

25

pulses of beans and chickpeas and pepper. The limited agricultural potential of the *Kebele* can be seen from the absence of other high value crops, such as fruits and vegetables, oilseeds and lentils, and also very limited presence of pepper cultivation. Widespread frost and dew cover limit the cultivation of high value crops.

Table 5: Major Land Use Patterns in Weheni Durbete *Kebele* by Different Crops

Land use system	Coverage (HA)
All annual crops (2010 *meher*)	**1354.2**
• Maize	510.6
• Finger millet	242.0
• Barley	174.0
• Teff	165.5
• Wheat	125.0
• Beans	109.0
• Pepper	22.3
• Chickpeas	5.8
Grazing	**125.0**
Forestland (Planted and natural)	**38.0**
Wasteland	**10.0**

SOURCE: Weheni Durbete *Kebele* Farmer Training Center, August 2010

The *Kebele* has a farmer training center (FTC). Unfortunately, the FTC is not well furnished in terms of benches and training manuals. The physical condition of the FTC is poor as compared with the FTCs in the other two study *kebeles*. According to the head of the FTC and the DA of the *Kebele*, the FTC does not have enough land and as a result does not generate income by renting land to farmers. This limits the possibility of enhancing the infrastructure of the FTC using local resources. The FTC is located in half-hectare of moderately fertile land that can only be used for demonstration of new technologies such as zero-tillage or new forage grass. It should be, however, noted that ecological disadvantage (high population pressure in this case) is also reinforced by administrative neglect as reflected in the lack of material support to the FTC.

The participation of the *Kebele* residents in the government-run extension package program is limited to purchase of chemical fertilizers and seeds. With limited means to afford the rising cost of fertilizers, the farmers complained about their growing dependence on external inputs as the land has become unable to produce without chemical fertilizers. In addition, there is some limited participation in other types of extension packages, such as sheep fattening, oxen fattening and modern beehives. The interviewed farmers clearly understand that their productivity potential is constrained by the *dega* agro-ecology and shortage of land.

In an environment where the opportunity to be a farm hero/heroine is limited, the *Kebele* has only 47 model farmers – that is, one in every 27 farm household is a model farmer. They are model farmers when compared to fellow farmers in their own community but none of them won any prize so far. According to the *Kebele* DA, most of them are model farmers in the sense of following the correct application of chemical fertilizers and seeds. A 50 year old widowed model farmer indicated that she was recently named a model farmer, though she has never received any training (except general information about extension packages after church on Sundays). Moreover, she has no income sources other than cereal farming – no gardening activity, no fruits, no high value crops such as pepper, lentils and onions. The good thing is that her 8-member household is food secure throughout the year and she attributes this to her hard work and contributions from her 7 children, all of whom except one have attained some kind of education, from elementary to college level.

3.5.2   *Ziyew Shiwun Kebele*

Ziyew *Shiwun Kebele* is found south of Bure *Woreda* along the Bure-Nekemte road at a distance of 27 km from Bure town. It is a *woinadega Kebele* having common borders with Fetam Sentom in the south, Fezele *Kebele* in the north, Gedam Lejamor in the east and Webberima *Woreda* in the west. The *Kebele* has Kuch town as its trade center and is favored by its location on the main road. The town seems to be a striving rural center that handles more than a dozen of trucks daily to transport agricultural goods not to mention the availability of public transport to Kuch and passing through it.

As shown in Table 3, Ziyew Shiwun is a relatively bigger *Kebele* of 37.1 km^2 twice the size of Weheni Durbete. The *Kebele* has 7675 residents supported by 1329 households. Compared to the *dega Kebele* of Weheni Durbete, Ziyew Shiwun is sparsely populated with a population density of 207 persons per km^2. Average landholding in the *Kebele* is 1.5 ha – this means that farm households in Ziyew Shiwun have as much as twice access to farmland compared to those in Weheni Durbete. This aided by *woinadega* agro-ecology leads to greater diversification in the cultivation of crops. This is also supported by diverse and greater livestock ownership in the *woinadega*.

The land use pattern in Ziyew Shiwun *Kebele* is characterized by cultivation of annual crops, grazing, forests (both planted and natural forests) as well as land for construction, especially in and around Kuch town (Table 6). The forest cover (both planted and natural forests) is encouraging as it can be seen from the size of the land, though a good part of it is planted with eucalyptus trees.

Table 6: Major Land use Systems in Ziyew Shiwun *Kebele*

Type of land use	Coverage (HA)
All annual crops (2010 *meher*)	**2219**
• Maize	747
• Wheat	650
• Pepper	198
• Teff	167
• Finger millet	145
• Chick pea	138
• Faba bean	106
• Bean	68
Grazing land	**160**
Forestland (planted & natural forest)	**600**
Bushland	**72**
Built up area	**120**
Wasteland	**20**

SOURCE: Ziyew Shiwun *Kebele* Farmer-Training Center, Kuch, August 2010.

As can be seen from Table 6, 2219 hectares of land is devoted to the production of annual crops. Major crops include maize, wheat, pepper, teff, finger millet, chickpeas, haricot bean and beans. These crops covered 747, 650, 198, 167, 145, 138, 108 and 68 ha of land respectively during the 2009 *meher* season. Ziyew Shiwun is located in one of the fertile plains in Bure *Woreda* with average crop yield of 79 quintals for maize and 61 for wheat.

There is a farmer-training center and one DA office adjacent to the FTC just east of Kuch town. The FTC is furnished with benches, training manuals, blackboard and thanks to the support provided by the Improving Productivity & Market Success (IPMS) project, a computer is also available. The building is plastered with mud and covered with corrugated iron. The FTC is located on one hectare of land, a small part of it is used to grow fodder for demonstration and a major part is rented and the proceeds are used to support the activities of the FTC and the extension program in general.

Because the *Kebele* has good agricultural productivity, extension work is given a very serious attention. We observed this during our visits to the FTC to conduct interviews, and in one occasion the DA left a message informing us that he went out to visit farmers who are participating in maize seed multiplication project. The message was found in a paper-made pigeonhole hanging on the DA's office door. Another DA also left a similar message informing his visitors that he had to be away for extension work. We thought this was a very clever way to inform the whereabouts of DAs to their clients. The fact that the DA cancelled a scheduled meeting with us in order to provide assistance to farmers about new technologies, such as multiplication maize seeds and others, show how DAs are serious about their work.

According to the DA, most farmers in Ziyew Shiwun are willing (a good number of them on their own initiative) to participate in the different types of packages supported by the extension service. Such crop packages as maize, wheat and teff are widely practiced in the area. For instance, a group of farmers who were selected to participate in a maize seed multiplication project during the 2010 *meher* season expect to reap the benefits of higher prices, which could be as much as three times the price of common maize used for consumption. Favored by the *Kebele*'s ecological endowments, there is a diversified cropping pattern in the extension program, such as fruits and vegetables packages (38 households) and seedling package, animal fattening, beehives and poultry packages (198 households).

According to information obtained from the DA office, there are 84 model farmers in Ziyew Shiwun. This means that one in every 16 farm household is a model farmer. Three model farmers of the *kebele* won prizes at the regional level in 2006/07, 2007/08 and 2008/09.

There are substantive changes in the lives of model farmers in the *kebele*. For instance, one of the model farmers that we interviewed (age 33) clearly revealed his modest beginning and his current aspiration to become a business leader in the community. Brought up by a single-parent (mother), the interviewed model farmer started his farming career with half hectare of land some ten years back. Over the years, he has expanded his farm by renting 5 ha of land from other farmers. In 2010 *meher* season, he has planted almost every kind of crop that grows in the area ranging from cereals, fruits and vegetable to pulses, oilseeds, onion, pepper and *gesho*.[14] He bought and applied 9 quintals of chemical fertilizers (DAP and urea). He has devoted 1.75 ha of his land to maize seed multiplication project.

More importantly, the model farmer keeps books of accounts of his costs and returns in the absence of which it would be difficult to make such big financial expenditures. He plans to build a house in Kuch town and expand his farm business by opening his access to *qolla* land (by means of rent) so that he can grow such high value crop as sesame. It is our conviction that such model farmers represent the typical model farmer that is described throughout this report.

3.5.3 Fetam Sentom Kebele

This is the most southerly *kebele* of the Bure *Woreda* stretching to the Abbay Gorge and touching the Bure-Nekemte Abbay Bridge and hence connecting the *woreda* to East Wellega zone of the Oromiya region. It has borders with Ziyew Shiwun and Gedem Lejamor in the north, Webberima *Woreda* in the west and Beko Tabo in the southwest and the Abbay River in the east and south. Although some parts of the *Kebele* lies in the *woinadega* with elevations up to 2166 meters asl, it is largely *qolla* and has a low point of 773 meters asl along the Abbay River. Favored by escarpments and good vegetation cover, Fetam Sentom receives sufficient amount of rainfall ranging from 1366 mm to 1659 mm and temperature ranges 17-24 degree Celsius.

In terms of area, Fetam Sentom with a land size of 79.6 km^2 is the second largest *Kebele* in the *Woreda* preceded by the neighboring *qolla Kebele* of Beko Tabo (175 km^2). With a population of 7647 persons population density is relatively low; that is, 96 persons per km^2. There is enough cultivable land in the *Kebele* and land-stressed *woinadega* farmers are intensely competing for favors to win contracts from individual land renters. Being favored by the co-presence of both *woinadega* and *qolla* agro-ecologies, the *Kebele* is suitable for the cultivation of cereals especially in the *woinadega* and oilseeds, fruits and vegetable crops in the *qolla*. It is also favored by the availability of cultivable pasture and forestlands thereby creating more opportunities for farm expansion, bigger herd size and commercial exploitation of forest resources for timber and charcoal production and local building materials.

---

[14]Shiny-leaf Buckthorn, African shrub or small tree in the family *Rhamnaceae*, commonly used as hops.

The *Kebele*'s land use system is characterized by cropland (annual and perennial), grazing land, forest and bush land. As expected land used for the different categories of crops (cereals, pulses, oilseeds, fruits and vegetables) constitutes 31% of the *Kebele*'s area and this is followed by grazing (9.7%) and forest/bush land (6.1%). As has been mentioned, there is good vegetation cover in the *Kebele*, especially escarpments and less hospitable *qolla* – where human habitation has been difficult due to fear of malaria and other *qolla*-borne diseases.

The *Kebele* is suitable for the production of such cereals as (maize, wheat and teff), oilseeds (noug[15], sesame, haricot bean) and fruit crops (mango, papaya, orange). Maize accounts for 37% of the total land cultivated with annual crops during the 2010 *meher* season. As it can be seen from Table 7, pepper is the fourth important crop in terms of area coverage. Interviewed farmers also indicated that pepper production has been expanding in the last couple of years. As a result, teff plots are being increasingly used for pepper cultivation. The growing popularity of pepper among farmers is due to a recent price hikes in the market.

Table 7: Major Land Use Systems in Fetam Sentom *Kebele*

Type of land use	Coverage (HA)
All annual crops (2010 *meher*)	**2541**
• Maize	918
• Wheat	500
• Teff	360
• Pepper	208
• Sesame	180
• Haricot bean	120
• Faba bean	80
• Finger millet	75
• Noug	45
• Potato	5
Grazing land	**770**
Forestland (planted and natural forest)	**25**
Bush land	**4060**
Wasteland	**112**

SOURCE: Fetam Sentom *Kebele* DA office.

---

[15] *Guizotia abyssinica*, an oil-seed crop, indigenous to Ethiopia.

Like the previous two study *Kebeles,* a farmer training center has also been built in Fetam Sentom to provide training for farmers in various extension packages, such as natural resource management, crop and animal packages. Based on the information provided by the DA, who is also responsible for the FTC, two types of trainings are given to farmers. These are (1) short-term trainings that last from half day to 2-3 days and (2) long-term trainings lasting 3-6 months. Examples of the former include BBM (Broad-Bed Maker) application, seed multiplication, fruit and vegetable grafting, animal fattening and soil and water conservation activities. In 2009/10, a total of 972 farmers received training in these activities. Examples of long-term training include crop, animal and bee production packages and some 40 farmers have been trained in 2009/10.

Generally, the extension program seems to be well-received by the farmers in Fetam Sentom. This can be seen from the number of model farmers – 333 (out of whom 6 are females) out of the total 1188 farm households in the *Kebele* about 28% are headed by model farmers. Three model farmers have won prizes at the Amhara region farmers' festival. Participation in maize, wheat and teff packages does not require any persuasion from the DAs as farmers have acquired sufficient experience and recognized the value of following the DA's instructions in the application of the package of recommendations.

The interviewed farmers admitted that there was a marked difference between the plots which were cultivated following the recommendation of DAs and those without. In the former there is better amount of yield. As a result, farmers are increasingly becoming conscious (and some have learned from their own experiences) of the fact that those who were cheating the 'packages' paid the price. For instance, temptations to reduce amount of fertilizer from the specified application significantly reduces returns.

4. Factors Influencing Farmer Entrepreneurship in Bure *Woreda*

A common approach in studying entrepreneurship of any kind is to focus on the personal traits and experiences of the individual entrepreneur. In other words, studying managerial, technical, entrepreneurial and inter-personal and social skills of entrepreneurs (as defined in Figure 1) provides important insights about the very idea of entrepreneurship. After all, entrepreneurship entails the taking of initiatives by individual actors, thus attracting our attention to the experiences of actual persons from whom lessons can be learnt. However, personality traits are not the only, and at times, even the most important factors for entrepreneurial success. This is particularly true of Ethiopian peasant farmers, who for ages ceaselessly encountered natural and manmade burdens that stifle chances of self-improvement and innovation.

In addition to the problems mentioned above, a second category of variables which can be collectively subsumed under the term 'contextual factors' – those factors that do not emanate from and are not a result of the experiences of individual actors *per se*, but operate at various levels of their socio-economic environment affect entrepreneurship. In the context of Ethiopian peasant farmers, these include social networks and support structures; availability of finance; physical resources and infrastructure; national policies and regional programs related to agricultural development, microfinance, cooperatives development, and health extension; local efforts and development interventions related to agricultural intensification, market orientation, as well as security and justice; NGO activities; and other local level factors, such as shifts in community attitudes.

The sub-sections that follow present the findings of the study in relation to the afore-mentioned factors of entrepreneurship based on data collected from model farmers, non-model farmers, other community members, development workers as well as from secondary materials.

4.1 Personal Factors

A range of personality factors impacting entrepreneurial activities of model farmers were identified by this study. Foremost among these are factors related to the character of individuals including early adoption of technology, risk taking behaviour, identifying opportunities, competitiveness, and farsightedness; followed by those factors that are experiential in origin. Childhood experiences; knowledge, skill, and habits garnered as sharecropper; outside experiences; and formal education all fall under the second category of personality factors. These attributes are related to the entrepreneurial, technical, managerial and personal maturity and social responsibility skill sets that are identified and described in the conceptual framework of section 2.6.

4.1.1 Individual Traits

Early adoption of agricultural technology was the most frequently cited characteristic feature of model farmers across the board. Accordingly, they are often described by community members as people who embrace eagerly agricultural technology introduced by development workers and experiment with it, often making adjustments so that the new technology fits their needs and capacities. The same sentiment is shared by agricultural development workers who describe model farmers as those at the forefront in the utilization of agricultural extension services. Unlike others, model farmers are not suspicious of new technology. Several examples of such behavior were identified by community members and development workers alike. In this regard, a model farmer in Weheni Durbete *kebele*, who is known for early adoption of technology, is a good example. According to key informants, this farmer was one of the first to adopt modern beehives introduced by the *woreda* agriculture and rural development office and significantly benefited from the adoption of the new technology. Afterwards, when the price of modern beehives went up, the farmer himself started to build beehives by imitating the modern beehives supplied by the government from locally available materials, a practice which is now common in the study area. Another model farmer in Ziyew Shiwun describes the situation in his own words as follows:

> *I am quick at adopting new technologies and ways of working. For instance, when BH 660 (improved maize variety) was first introduced in our woreda, I was one of the first ten farmers in the kebele to adopt it. As you know, we farmers do not take up new things fast. Back then, the majority of farmers in our kebele refused to use BH 660. In fact, one of my sharecroppers left me fearing that the harvest from the improved variety is not edible by humans.*

Even though early adoption carries its own risk, for instance, loss of harvest due to drought or lack of sustainable supply of inputs, it is said that it gives model farmers a comparative advantage as it allows them to accumulate experience and, most of all, if successful, increase productivity and build their capital assets which they can use for other endeavors.

The second important feature of most model farmers is the tendency to identify opportunities of making money both on and off the farm. This tendency may take the form of reading telltale signs of change in the price of agricultural products or increased demand for certain agricultural produce. Among model farmers, this feature is often found in combination with another personal tendency, namely, the propensity to take risk in making decisions about use of such opportunities. Of course, this is neither to say that model farmers constantly venture into activities that entail so much risk as to threaten their livelihood, nor is it to say that non-model farmers do not take risks in order to reap potential benefits. Rather, data gathered from the field show that model farmers take risks more frequently than non-model farmers. What is more important here is that this risk taking tendency is displayed by model farmers of all economic backgrounds and across the different agro-ecology zones, though *woinadega* model farmers tend to be more daring because of availability of more opportunities than, especially, *dega* model farmers.

The study's attempt at identifying the personal characters of model farmers has also uncovered a third important feature, the spirit of competitiveness. When asked what derives them to success, almost all of the interviewed model farmers pointed to the fact that they have a very competitive spirit. This competitiveness is reflected not only in their desire to match or surpass the level of success reached by other farmers but also in their ambition to achieve high standards of success they set for themselves. A model farmer in Ziyew Shiwun says:

> *I am a very hardworking man. I always compare what I achieved the current year with my achievement last year. Often I see improvement. But that improvement by itself does not satisfy me. I again ask myself 'why can not I reach where X or Y has reached? It is this feeling that prevents me from becoming fully satisfied with what I have now and always spurs me forward.*

Similarly, another model farmer in Fetam Sentom *kebele* illustrates his feeling regarding the reason behind his thriving farming and other business activities as follows:

> *Since my childhood, I was very competitive and very much disliked being defeated at anything, even in games. That feeling has followed me to my adulthood and is still very much a reason for my success. Of course, I'm now better than almost all farmers in the kebele in terms of farm productivity as well as asset ownership. However, I have my own goal of becoming an investor competing at the regional level.*

Farsightedness and forward planning traits are additional personal characteristic features of successful farmers. It was stressed that model farmers apply these skills not only in relation to farming and other business activities but also in social life. Some of the model farmers interviewed keep books of accounting to monitor their income and expenditure. The DAs in the study *kebele* also told us that a few model farmers sit with them to plan their farming activities, including what and when to plant. Moreover, the study found that, as a result of their farsightedness and forward planning skills, model farmers often escape disasters that befall on other farmers and refrain from asset eroding practices such as grain loan, and borrowing cash from illegal money lenders at exorbitant interest rates.

4.1.2 Experience Related Factors

A successful farmer possesses a number of skills in addition to the basic knowledge of farming. In fact, the most important factor that accounts for the success of model farmers is the possession of some key managerial skills (identified in the conceptual framework), such as labor management, planning, and some elementary bookkeeping (e.g. registering expenses and sales).

While most of the interviewed model farmers have a more or less similar household composition with other community members, they are often praised for their efficient management of household labour. They also make efficient decisions when they hire additional labour. It is not uncommon to hear in the study localities that a model farmer's management of household labour matches that of a business enterprise. Asked about their labour management strategy, most model farmers stated that they routinely divide tasks by age and sex and follow up their proper execution. This is even true of their management of employed labour. Interviewed model farmers stated that they m   anage the daily laborers they employ for seasonal work as well as their sharecroppers in a manner that is not open for labour wastage. This would help minimize unnecessary extension of work. A model farmer in Fetam Sentom elaborates his style of labour management by saying:

> Unlike other farmers, I calculate how many farm hand I need for the day or weak and employ only that many workers, no more no less. If I employ more than necessary, I waste my money; and if less are employed, the completion of one task will be delayed and overlap with another that has to be done at a particular time. In addition, when I shed workers, I do not do it abruptly, for I may need them for one task or another. Rather, I let them go a few at a time.

A uniquely developed skill for planning is another valuable skill that sets model farmers apart from their other colleagues. In this respect, model farmers carefully plan their on and off-farm activities. According to Development Agents in the study areas, model farmers not only have detailed and clear cut plans for different aspects of their lives but also stick to the extent possible to their plans.

In addition to planning, another factor that explains the success of model farmers is their practice in cost-benefit analysis. According to the model farmers interviewed for this study, they do not venture into any on-or off-farm venture without studying its costs and benefits. For instance, model farmers who produce cereals keep track of their expenses starting from land preparation to harvesting and finally compare their expenses with the return. This, they say, helps them decide whether to continue cultivating the same cereal on the same land size, expand the production of the cereal, reduce the amount of land covered by the cereal, or even totally cease the production of that particular cereal. The same applies to off-farm activities, such as house renting or grain trade.

An important issue that needs to be addressed here is the source of managerial skills exhibited by model farmers. One of the key findings of this study has been the immense role that formal education plays in building managerial skills by model farmers. For instance, a model farmer in one of the focus group discussions said that being able to read, write and do arithmetic are key factors that explain his managerial skills. He furthermore said, *having formal education is like having a parent who is always by your side. They both are there for a person in times of need.* Focus group discussions with community members conducted in all the three study *kebeles* revealed that most model farmers have attained some formal education (see profile of model farmers, ***Annex III***).

In addition to formal education, experience acquired as sharecropper was provided as another source of managerial skills by model farmers. Given the humble origins of most model farmers, this should come as no surprise. Most of the interviewed model farmers stated that the several years they spent as sharecroppers have taught them not only to hard work, but also the need to manage resources, plan ahead, and calculate gains and losses. This is stressed especially by those who started their career as farm laborers or sharecroppers[16] at a young age. Model farmers who underwent this process describe sharecropping as a period of apprenticeship/training towards independent farming. The sharecropping experience is still valuable for young farmers.

---

[16] These are mostly farmers who worked under the control and management of experienced and relatively better off farmers and were entitled to receive up to one-fourth of the produce of a given harvest.

Case 1: Farm Apprenticeship as a Factor for the Success of Model Farmers

A successful 50-year old farmer from Fetam Sentom started his farming career as an apprentice. He was hired as a farm laborer at the age of 21 and worked for 7 years before starting his own farm. Working an apprentice helped him learn not only the nitty-gritty of farming but also about good farm management. Presently, in addition to the 3 ha of land that he owns, he often rents up to 2.75 hectares of land. Each hectare of land cost him between 3200 to 4000 birr. In 2010 *meher* season he applied 10.5 quintals of fertilizer and planted more than 5 ha of land with tef, wheat, maize, red pepper, chickpea and oilseeds. He expected to harvest between 120 and 140 quintals. His 9-member household provides sufficient source of farm labor, two of his sons are share-croppers and three other children are in school.

He was trained in compost production, fertilizer use, and primary health care through the health extension package. He indicated that the secret of good farming is timely preparation, planting, weeding and harvesting of crops and proper application of chemical fertilizers in accordance with the recommendation given by the DA. His experience as an apprentice in a hard-working farm household also helped him to value hard work and motivated him to be successful when he started working for himself. In addition to crop production, he earns income by growing *Gesho* (500 trees), house rental (200 birr from 2 houses per month) by renting mule cart and by selling eucalyptus tree (he has cultivated 2000 trees).

Another factor that was stated by model farmers as a source of the valuable skills that they have is their upbringing. Many of them stress the fact that they inherited good work habits and accumulated knowledge of their parents. The fact that they were assigned certain duties that fitted their age and skill during their childhood by their parents inculcated in them a sense of responsibility and disposition to hard work. In the words of one model farmer in Weheni Durbete *kebele*: *I learnt hard work, proper use of resources, such as money, land, water, labour, farm byproducts, and farm inputs from my father, who was a farmer well known for his success.*

Finally, some form of prior non-farm engagement was found to aid in the acquisition of skills that account for farmer success in on-and off-farm activities. Four instances of non-farm engagements were identified by the research as external experiences that contribute to the success of model farmers. These include employment as a migrant laborer in urban areas, self employment in the market sector, and some experience in local administration and in the army.

The first two forms of non-farm experience were corroborated by the narratives of two model farmers in Weheni Durbete and Fetam Sentom *kebeles*. Out of the need for survival, both farmers left their villages and moved to nearby towns –

the first one was employed as a daily labourer in a grain market, and the second as a shoe-shine boy. Their experience in the small towns helped them develop skills to calculate gains and losses and plan ahead for tomorrow in the face of uncertainty. These skills became valuable when they returned back to their villages to farm.

The third form of non-farm engagement, i.e. involvement in local administration, was raised by both model farmers and other community members as a source of some of the skills possessed by the former. This exposes the farmer to new ideas and opens the door for many training opportunities and conferences. Most importantly, experience in the local administration introduces the famer to the workings of a formal organization. The skills that a farmer learns from this experience could be used in his/her on-and off-farm endeavors.

The study attempted to see if the success of model farmers who were involved in local administration can be linked to unfair practices (such as land grabbing) or other questionable activities. In two of the study *kebeles* the responses obtained were negative. In the third, a respondent expressed his suspicion that one of the model farmers in the *kebele* might have unlawfully taken money and property when the farmers' cooperative he headed was dissolved following the fall of the Derg and used that as start-up capital. We could not, however, corroborate such views. Regarding the issue of land size, the model farmers in the study *kebeles* have plots that are more or less similar to the average household possession.

Last is the case of the model farmer in Ziyew Shiwun, who served in the Ethiopian National Defense Forces during the Ethio-Eritrean war (1998-2000) and was honorably discharged at the end of the war. According to him, the few years he spent in the army were eye opening. He elaborated his experience as follows:

> *I have seen different kinds of people during my stay in the army. I have seen good and bad people, savers and spenders, etc. As a result, I learnt a lot from others and was able to lead my life properly. Moreover, my assignment in the personnel section of my division has given me the opportunity to learn from my co-workers and superiors.*

In sum, it is important to acknowledge that non-farm engagements, often outside the locality of the model farmers, play the additional role in providing the startup or add-on capital that is much needed by farmers to engage in entrepreneurial activities.

4.2 Contextual Factors

4.2.1 Community Attitude

For people to start and run new businesses or, in the agricultural sector, to try and intensify and diversify their existing farming operations, there has to be at least some community support for entrepreneurial activities. Moreover, community members have to acknowledge and celebrate the achievements of others if people are to be encouraged to work hard, take risks and seek opportunities to improve their lives. In light of this, the study examined community attitudes towards innovation, adoption of new technologies, entrepreneurship, and personal success in the study *kebeles*.

Responses obtained from model farmers as well as other community members in this regard show that there is undeniably favorable change in community attitudes towards success. Model farmers are being seen as socially responsible community members (a factor related to the personal maturity and social responsibility skill set described in the conceptual framework in section 2.6) who not only support their families but also positively influence other farmers. It was found that farmers who work hard and improve their living standards are praised and respected by others. An informant in Fetam Sentom elaborates this as follows:

> *Even though there are still some people who are jealous of these [model] farmers, the majority of the community appreciates them. In the past, successful farmers used to be called "wesage", that is someone who takes the property of others through evil means. But presently people positively recognize the successes of hardworking farmers. Successful farmers, on their part, not only share with other farmers the sources of their achievements but also advise them to do the same.*

In short, the successes of model farmers encourage others to follow in their footsteps (further discussion on this point will be made in the next section).

4.2.2 Social Networks

Farmer entrepreneurs are not solitary actors whose successes or failures are determined by their personal qualities alone. Rather, they rely on a number of other factors to realize their entrepreneurial ambitions. Chief among these are social networks. According to community members interviewed in the field, model farmers have robust social networks that contribute to their on- and off-farm endeavors. In this respect, some model farmers identified people in their social networks as role models are sources of business advice and information and other resources. Moreover, information gathered from the field attests that social networks of various sorts have been used as sources of initial capital for on-and off-farm ventures. For instance, in all of the three study *kebeles*, it was stressed by community members that many model farmers received some kind of financial assistance from their godfathers (*yekirestina abat*) at the initial stages of their farming careers.

4.2.3 Access to Finance

Realizing one's entrepreneurial ambition requires access to financial resources. In this respect, peasant farmer entrepreneurs need finance to intensify and diversity their farm activities and to start and expand their off-farm ventures. In addition to financial support from their social networks, farmers take loans from various sources. There are intermittent small loans that are provided by NGOs and/or bilateral organizations to farmers in the study areas through the *Woreda* Agriculture and Rural Development Office. Model farmers do not appreciate these loans. They were small in amount and erratic in availability. Moreover, as they did not involve serious obligation to payback, their impact was limited. Recently, the most important sources of finance for farmers are the various saving and credit associations and cooperatives. The Amhara Credit and Saving Institution (ACSI) has become a dominant player in the provision of credit and other financial services to rural areas. A significant majority of the model farmers in the study areas use the services of these organizations. Model farmers, for instance, use the credit facilities of these organizations to purchase farm inputs and to start off-farm businesses like livestock and grain trading.

The study attempted to assess availability of finance and its utilization by model farmers by conducting interviews with the head of ACSI Bure branch office and the *Woreda* Cooperatives Organizing and Promotion office. According to the first interviewee, the major areas for which the ACSI provides loans include purchase of farm inputs (like plough oxen, fertilizers and others), startup capital for small businesses and expansion of small scale irrigation. Out of the 7515 active clients that the ACSI has in the Bure *woreda*, 6902 (92%) are farmers. Quite a few of the farmers who started taking loan for simple agricultural purposes, according to the official of the ACSI, prospered and moved on to other businesses. These farmers, he added, are hard working, accept the advice of professionals and diversify their activities. It was found that the organization also provides technical and business advice to customers to build their capacity. The group-guarantee scheme that the ACSI uses in the provision of loans has helped broaden the opportunity for getting loans for many farmers.[17]

---

[17] The study has made an attempt to know the number of model farmers who are clients of ACSI. However, we have learned that ACSI does not use the model/non-model distinction as a criterion for administering its loans and hence the information on this issue was not available.

According to an informant from the *woreda* cooperatives organizing and promotion office, there are some 30 cooperatives, 13 of which are engaged in saving and credit. The 13 saving and credit associations, which have 1054 members, provide credit services at a limited scale.

4.2.4 Resources

One of the objectives of the study was to see if access to resources (such as water logged land, land fertility and others) set apart model farmers from the rest of the farming community and contribute to their successes. The study found that the size and fertility of the farming land of model farmers is by and large similar with that of the other farmers. Similarly, model farmers do not seem to be at an advantage in terms of access to water and transportation services. In this respect, interviewed community members, FGD participants and key informants uniformly stated that there are not significant variations regarding plot size and fertility between model farmers and others. According to one informant in Weheni Durbete *kebele,* even if such differences prevail today, they are results of the hard work of the model farmers instead of initial differences. In fact, one of the distinctive qualities of model farmers is their propensity to increase the size and number of plots they cultivate through land rent. They rent land from other farmers, usually women, the elderly and lazy farmers. Almost all of the interviewed model farmers (except those in Weheni Durbete where the opportunity for land rent is almost non-existent) indicated that they have rented two or more plots on average. For instance, some model farmers increased the size of their plots by more than 150% during the 2010 *meher* season. Model farmers venture into land rental activities as they have the confidence that they will return their investment through hard work and increased productivity (see Section 5.1.1 for details).

4.2.5 Agricultural Extension Services

One of the qualities of model farmers is the level of utilization of extension services, which is not often matched by non-model farmers. The study attempted to see if agricultural extension services in the *woreda* are indeed conducive for farmer entrepreneurship as characterized by intensification, diversification, and shift to off-farm ventures. The extension package that was being largely implemented in the *woreda* (and the region as a whole) during the study period is known as the minimum extension package. Its main objective is to increase productivity and production of cereal crops in order to assure food self-sustainability in the region. Moreover, the package aims at increasing household income through horticulture, livestock rearing and agro-forestry.

In each of the study *kebeles*, there are agricultural development stations manned by three professionals, each trained in crop production and protection, animal production, and natural resource development. These DAs work on a day-to-day basis with the farmers. One of the DAs also serves as the station coordinator for the development station and the FTC. Interviews with model farmers showed that these DAs meet frequently with farmers (even more so with the model ones) and provide on-farm advice and training. In fact, interviewed model farmers attribute a significant portion of their success to the efforts of current and previous DAs.

An important factor that needs to be raised here is the role of some hardworking DAs in the success of model farmers. Two model farmers, one in Ziyew Shiwun and another in Fetam Sentom, cited the DAs in their respective *kebeles* who worked diligently in order to transform the lives of farmers in the *kebele* in which they worked. A model farmer in Fetam Sentom explains this as follows:

> *There was a DA in our kebele by the name of Kumsa. I can say that his efforts are the starting point of my success. One day, he came to my plot and told me that he needed to talk to me. After I told him that I would go to his office that afternoon, he departed. When we met in his office, he told me that he wants me to try improved farming techniques. Together we sat and prepared a plan which contained information about what I will plant on which plot. After that, he visited my plots and even worked with me. Seeing how the productivity of my plots has increased, I continued to work hard following what he taught me.*

Another model farmer in Ziyew Shiwun stated that he started to engage in off-farm activities, such as apiculture and livestock fattening, in response to the repeated advice he got from a DA in the *kebele* regarding the need for diversification. These activities, which are market oriented and have the core objective of making profit, he argues, have significantly improved his economic standing in the community.

Farmer training centers (FTCs) are an integral part of the agricultural extension services in the study areas. Out of the 19 *kebeles* in the Bure Zuria *Woreda*, 17 have operational FTCs and 2 have FTCs that are still under construction. Each agricultural development station has an FTC with a class room and demonstration plots. Almost all of the interviewed model farmers and several of the non-model farmers have received training in these FTCs. According to interviews with coordinators of the agricultural development stations of the study *kebeles*, the FTCs provide trainings aimed at familiarizing farmers with modern agricultural technologies and make them business oriented. For example, they provide lessons that encourage farmers to cultivate high-value, marketable crops, such as producing red pepper. They also advise farmers to diversify their livelihoods by undertaking various income generating activities, such as poultry farming, bee keeping, agro-forestry (e.g. growing eucalyptus trees for sale); and growing crops twice a year when opportunity for irrigation exists and so forth. Extension packages and trainings provided by FTCs not only expose farmers to locally available opportunities but also promote farming as a business enterprise.

In addition to providing training, FTCs permanently display technological inputs, such as rope pumps, bee hives and roof water harvesting techniques. The role of FTCs in encouraging farmer entrepreneurship cannot be overstated in light of the success of some of them in transmitting knowledge and skills that help in agricultural intensification and diversification.

Of course, the strength of FTCs in the study *kebeles* varies. For example, the FTC in Fetam Sentom is relatively well equipped and most active because of the support it received from the IMPS project. According to the coordinator of the agricultural development station, training on crop production, animal resources development and natural resources management were given to 60 and 40 farmers in 2008/09 and in 2009/10 respectively. Moreover, several additional short trainings were provided for farmers in the *kebele* in 2009/10. The table below provides data on the type of trainings and number of participants.

Table 8: Training Topics and Number of Participants in Trainings Provided in Fetam Sentom FTC in 2009/10

Topic of Training	Number of Participants
Vertisol drainage and use of BBM	263
Improved maize seed multiplication	128
Natural resource management	158
Horticulture	200
Livestock fattening	223
Total	**972**

SOURCE: Field Data

The FTC in Ziyew Shiwun, which is relatively well furnished, provides various trainings for farmers. According to the DA working in the *kebele*, in 2009/10, 24 farmers were trained on crop production, and 20 each in nursery establishment and fattening. The FTC in Weheni Durbete is inadequately furnished and was not supported by the IPMS project (see below for the details). It also suffers from shortage of land for demonstration. Yet, it provides skill oriented trainings to farmers. For example, in 2009/10 it trained 40 farmers in crop production.

It is important to indicate here that entrepreneurial and business development trainings were not offered by the FTCs in the study *kebeles*. However, some of the trainings indirectly address the above issues. For instance, trainees are often encouraged to develop a business plan regarding their farm activities and also to keep track of their farm related expenses, both of which are important elements of entrepreneurial activity as indicated the in conceptual model (Figure 1).

4.2.6 Health Extension Services

The health status of farmers and their family members is undoubtedly crucial to their success. As farmers primarily rely on household labour ensuring health at the household level is very important. This need is to some extent met by the health extension program, which constitutes 12 health care activities[18] to be implemented by health extension workers at the *kebele* level. In each *kebele* there is a health extension worker, invariably females, who are working with women to improve their home management and their personal as well as family hygiene. Health extension workers also closely work with DAs and participate in the selection of model farmers based on their performance in the health extension package.

4.2.7 Cooperatives

Cooperatives in the study *kebeles* were discussed above in relation to their loan provision activities. Their contribution to the success of model farmers, however, goes beyond that. The task of organizing and assisting cooperatives in the region is in the hands of the Amhara National Regional State Cooperatives Promotion Agency, which, as of 2008/09 has overseen the establishment of 5,977 cooperatives on 19 different lines of work including multipurpose, saving and credit and service. Returning to the study *woreda*, there are some 30 cooperatives in the *woreda* with a total membership of 11,257, and all save one have been profitable and have paid dividends to their members.

Asked about the benefit they get from the cooperatives, in which most cases they are founding members, the interviewed model farmers stated that they have been able to sell their produce for better prices and with no fear of being cheated.

---

[18] These include constructing a pit latrine, preparing and using a hand washing facility, vaccination of mothers and children, constructing a separate enclosure for animals, construction a shelf for household utensils, using improved/fuel saving stove, storing water in a jerry can with a narrow mouth, using bed net, having a house with a window, proper solid waste disposal, proper liquid waste disposal, and proper clothing.

Moreover, they stated that their access to farm inputs, market information, and credit has increased significantly after joining the cooperatives They also indicated that membership in a cooperative has taught them how to save and when and for what purpose to borrow.

4.2.8 Law and Order

The general level of law and order prevailing in the study areas is one factor accounting for greater success of model farmers. Model farmers and other community members stressed that there was an additional incentive to work harder and invest in on-farm as well as off-farm ventures since there is greater sense of security regarding one's own property. Comparing the current situation with that of the Derg, informants explained that the right to sell one's produce at market price and whenever and wherever one wants is a source of motivation by itself. Moreover, better maintenance of law and order at the local level, resulting from community policing activities and community involvement in the form of neighborhood councils and social courts, has provided as an additional factor for farmer entrepreneurship.

4.3   National Projects

One objective of the study was to see which national programs have provided support for the development of farmer entrepreneurship in the study region in general and the localities in particular. Interviews with officials from the regional agriculture and rural development bureau revealed that there indeed are many such projects in the region. The first one of such initiatives is the rural capacity building project, which is being undertaken in 23 *woredas* (including the study *woreda*) of the region. The project aims to strengthen agricultural extension services and to make them responsive to farmers' need and facilitate the adoption of efficient agricultural technologies. It was further indicated by officials from the Bure Zuria Agriculture and Rural Development Office that the project provides training for professionals in various areas and works to popularize modern farming technology. Moreover, the project has provided assistance for 17 FTCs in the form of books, training modules, shelves, chairs and equipments for demonstration.

The second and probably the most important national factor as far as the study area is concerned is a project titled Improving Productivity & Market Success (IPMS) of Ethiopian Farmers. According to the project website, the project, which is funded by the Government of Canada through the Canadian International Development Agency (CIDA), is owned by the Ministry of Agriculture and Rural Development (MoARD) and is implemented by the

International Livestock Research Institute. The project has six focus areas, namely, knowledge management, capacity development, commodity development, gender, HIV/AIDS and environment. The contribution of this project to agricultural development efforts of the region is widely felt from the regional to the *kebele* levels by all stakeholders. Moreover, as Bure is one of the ten pilot *woredas* of the project, farmers have benefited significantly.

The project works vigorously to achieve market oriented agricultural development in the *woreda* in collaboration with the *woreda* office of agriculture and rural development. The assistance provided for two of the FTCs in the study *kebeles* (Ziyew Shiwun and Fetam Sentom) is specially worth mentioning as it has significantly improved the capacity of the FTCs (by supplying them with computers, printers, TVs, DVD Players, satellite dishes, books, teaching modules, demonstration materials, and generators for those without electric power). The DAs have also received in-service training in their areas of expertise. Training and demonstrations are also given to farmers through the FTCs, and study tours and field days were also organized. Moreover, the project is at the heart of most farmer entrepreneurial activities. Cattle and sheep fattening, poultry, apiculture, as well as horticulture (provision of grafted seedlings of mango, avocado, banana and papaya, and sugar cane) are all areas on which the IPMS project works, and through which model farmers have prospered.

Plate 2: FTC in Weheni Durbete *Kebele*

47

Plate 3: A relatively Well Equipped FTC in Fetam Sentom (Left) and Rope Pump Used for Demonstration in Ziyew Shiwun FTC (Right)

5. Entrepreneurial Measures, Challenges, and Prospects of Model Farmers

If lessons are to be drawn from the success stories of model farmers and their success are to be scaled up, the processes that they passed through need to be documented in detail. Moreover, sustaining their successes requires that the challenges of farmer entrepreneurship are uncovered and addressed through proper policy measures. The following sections deal with these topics in some detail.

5.1 Entrepreneurial Measures

The study's attempt to explore the entrepreneurial measures taken by model farmers in the study *kebeles* uncovered numerous and diverse measures each geared towards a common goal, namely profit maximization as an important entrepreneurial skill of model farmers. We have categorized these measures into four major groups of activities, namely: productivity and scaling up of production on the farm, on-farm diversification, supplementary agricultural diversification, and non-agricultural business ventures. Using case studies from the field, we shall discuss each of these in the following sections.

It is noteworthy here that, even though model farmers might have originally been engaged in subsistence agriculture primarily with the aim of sustaining their families throughout the year, that goal seems to have been satisfactorily met now. With better production and productivity, and food self sufficiency, model farmers have started to see their farm more as a business enterprise producing for the market in addition to its role as a source of food for household consumption. It is in this context that we look at the measures undertaken by model farmers in the study area.

5.1.1 Increasing Productivity, Scaling up Production, and Reducing Farming Cost

Model farmers take numerous measures (earlier, more frequently, and consistently than non-model farmers) to increase productivity of their plots. Moreover, they look for and grab opportunities of scaling up production through farm expansion. Below, we will look at some of these productivity-enhancing measures in greater detail.

Using improved seeds: model farmers emphasized that they use improved seeds of cereal crops as these are more productive and increase the amount of harvest that can be marketed. In doing so, they tend to follow DA advice in their use of improved seeds, in terms of both the quantity and quality of seeds applied.

49

Using chemical fertilizers: all of the interviewed model farmers stated that they use chemical fertilizers on their plots. They added that they follow proper instruction in the use of fertilizers, as opposed to many farmers who apply fertilizers far less than that recommended by the DA, or at inappropriate time. Explaining the situation, a model farmer stated that many farmers, thinking of the amount of money spent to buy the fertilizer, become sparing and apply too little on their plots. However, this practice does more harm than good as the amount applied results in very little tangible change in productivity, if any, and the money spent is not earned back. He concluded his explanation by saying *"the land will give you back, if you gave to it"*.

Preparing compost: one component of the agricultural extension package that is being aggressively pursued by development workers at all levels is the preparation of compost. The study found that most farmers (model and non-model alike) are currently preparing compost on their own compound from inputs available around the homestead. However, model farmers stated that they undertook the activity more seriously as soon as it was introduced and have benefited significantly as it increases soil fertility and thus productivity. Moreover, most interviewed model farmers stated that they usually exceed the DA requirement of the 20 m^2, as the compost they prepare can reduce their expense for chemical fertilizers, while at the same time increase crop production.

Rain water harvesting, use of rope and pedal pumps: rain water harvesting is one of the strategies pursued by some model farmers in the study area. This strategy, though not widely used partly because of technical difficulties in the preparation, is aimed at producing crops for household consumption in plots located in one's own backyard. In a very limited way, water harvesting seems to have made contributions by partly satisfying the consumption needs of peasant households and sparing harvest from other plots for marketing. In addition to rain water harvesting, model farmers use rope and pedal pumps to supply water to their plots and thereby increase production.

Minimum tillage (zero tillage): is a method of planting crops without plowing the field first. The technique involves leaving about 30% of harvest residue on the plot, allowing minimum disturbance of the field by humans and animals and then applying round up (a non-selective weed killer) on the plot to free it from any plant life. The seed is then sown on the plot tilled just once to prepare furrows for planting seed in the soil. Alternatively, one can prepare the furrow using a hoe. This is followed by the application of primagram gold (a pre-emergence herbicide effective against most annual grasses and broadleaf weeds) to prevent the growth of weeds. As the practice does not require repeated tilling and weeding, it significantly conserves labor expenses. The practice which was introduced by Sassakawa Global 2000 to Fetam Sentom *kebele* in 2005/06 with the involvement of 20 farmers is now widespread. According to informants, model farmers are known for taking up and continuing to use the technique. Moreover, interviews with model farmers revealed that by using the technique to produce maize and millet mainly for household consumption, they have been able to shift labour to increase the production of labour intensive cash crops like pepper[19]. The method is also found to be suited to the needs of farmers without oxen as it does not require land preparation using oxen power.

Vertisol management: as 17% of the study area is covered by vertisols, the proper management of vertisol plots is key for farmer success. The study found that model farmers are extensively engaged in vertisol drainage using the Broad-Bed Maker (BBM). For instance, in Fetam Sentom, one of the DAs interviewed estimated about 80% of the users of BBM are model farmers.

According to interviewed model farmers, since plots covered with vertisol suffer from water logging, productivity was extremely low on these plots. On locations where water logging is particularly high, plots were left uncultivated from the beginning of June to the middle of September until the water dries up and were usually sown with pulse crops. However, most of the interviewed model farmers were able to solve this problem and benefit from the increased productivity and double cropping by using BBM. The case below illustrates the above point.

---

[19] Note that the technique is stated to benefit poor and non-model farmers who do not own plow oxen (or own only one) and do not have household labour as they are able to engage in minimum tillage farming with little trouble.

Case 2: Vertisol Management Using BBM Technology

A 48 year-old model farmer in Fetam Sentom kebele has been using the BBM technology. When vertisol management with BBM was started in 2008/09 by providing 65 BBMs for the same number of farmers, he was one of the first adoptees (the BBMs cost 163 birr each and were provided in credit to be paid in three years). He farmed 1.75 hectares of vertisol land with the BBM and planted wheat in June. Working hard on the plots, he harvested 60 quintals of wheat per hectare. After harvesting the wheat, he planted the plots for the second time with pulse crops using the moisture that is left over. Thus, he was able to market bigger amounts of produce and earned more cash. In recognition of these and several other successful on-farm and off-farm ventures, he was selected as a model farmer from his community and received awards at the regional as well as national levels in 2006/07, 2007/08, and 2008/09.

Renting land: as already mentioned above, model farmers frequently engage in the renting of additional plots of land from other farmers within the *kebele* as well as in neighboring *kebeles*, and even across the regional border in *kebele*s located in East Wolega Zone of the Oromia National Regional State. It was found that model farmers rent plots of 0.5 – 2 hectares from other farmers in their locality with the aim of scaling up production (one farmer may rent plots from two or more farmers) often for a one year period. In addition to this, model farmers rent plots from schools and FTCs in their respective *kebeles*.

Large scale renting of land is carried out by model farmers in Fetam Sentom, who reported that they rent plots of 2-15 hectares in neighboring *qolla kebele* and in East Wolega. The practice seems to have intensified in recent years following the success of model farmers and the resulting increase in their financial capacity. In this regard, a 33 year-old model farmer interviewed in Ziyew Shiwun indicated that some three years ago he rented 2 *timads*[20] of land in the *kebele* and made profit from the teff he produced on the plots. Finding the venture profitable, he expanded his land renting activity to an adjacent *kebele*[21]. Currently, he has even gone as far as Wolega to rent farm land and produce on a

---

[20]Timad refers to the amount of land that can be plowed by a pair of oxen in a day and is approximately equivalent to quarter of a hectare.
[21] Note that this is possible under the Amhara National Regional State Rural Land Administration and Use System Implementation Regulation No. 51/2007 which doesn't put a limit on the amount of land that can be rented (Zikre- Hig Gazette No. 14, May 11, 2007)

much larger scale and plans to engage in commercial agriculture in the future (See *Annex IV* for size of land cultivated by model farmers and the corresponding amount of production in 2010 *Meher)*.

Moreover, unsatisfied with their current scale of production, all of the interviewed model farmers expressed their desire and readiness to rent more land and grow crops for the market. Coupled with increased productivity per unit area, expansion of farming plots has meant greater surplus production. Model farmers, particularly those who used the rented land to grow high value products, such as sesame, have been able to use the cash they earned as a start-up capital for non-agricultural ventures, which will be discussed below.

5.1.2 On-farm Diversification

On-farm diversification is used here to refer to diversification into agricultural activities that farmers did not traditionally engage in. In recognition of unmet demands and anticipation of high market price for certain items, model farmers in the study area often diversify (earlier than the average farmers) the crops they grow.

One common diversification activity that is practiced in the study areas is the planting of red pepper and sesame on plots that were used for the production of such crops as finger millet, maize and teff. The same can be said of the production of teff, which is becoming more popular in the traditionally barley growing *kebele* of Weheni Durbete. To this, we can add the cultivation various fruits, including papaya, mango, avocado, and banana, especially by farmers who have managed to tap water using pumps.

Another key activity that model farmers are largely engaged in is the multiplication of improved maize seeds. According to a crop seed multiplication professional from the Bure Zuraia *Woreda* office of agriculture and rural development, seed multiplication is an activity commonly undertaken by model farmers with plots suitable for the task as well as other non-model farmers who are known to be hardworking and early technology adopters with suitable plots. Multiplication of improved maize seeds was started in the *woreda* in the *meher* of 2010 in an arrangement whereby the Amhara Seed Enterprise and private investors enter a contractual agreement with farmers. A total of 489.25 hectares of land was used for seed multiplication in 7 *kebeles* of the *woreda*, including Ziyew Shiwun and Fetam Sentom. In spite of the extra care and labour requirement of the task, particularly during pollination, the venture seems to be quite profitable as the price for a quintal of improved maize seed in 2010 was 750 birr, while the price of maize for consumption in the same year was only about 200 birr. Even when we take an average productivity of 27.5 quintals of improved seed and 60 quintals of maize for consumption, there is a gross additional income of about 8625 birr per hectare of improved maize seed production. The only additional expense of seed multiplication being the extra labour during pollination.

5.1.3 Supplementary Agricultural Diversification

Interview results showed that model farmers engage in supplementary agricultural activities. Even though these activities are not as central and important as crop farming, their contribution to the success of model farmers cannot be understated. Most important of these supplementary activities are cattle and sheep fattening. According to model farmers, these activities are very much preferable because of the fact that both have high profit return and are short-term activities. For instance, an ox selected for fattening is fed from beginning of October to mid-December and then sold off. The net profit from the sale of a fattened ox can range from 2000 to 4000 birr, while a profit of 400 to 600 birr can be made from a fattened sheep. Even if cattle and sheep rearing and fattening are widely practiced by model and non-model farmers in the Bure *woreda,* the study findings showed that the tendency to sell livestock without fattening and to attempt fattening without adequate preparation (in terms of feed production and enclosing space for the animal/s to be fattened) are more common among non-model farmers. In contrast, model farmers engage in the fattening of animals more systematically and are able to become more profitable.

Growing *gesho* (shiny leaf buckthorn) and eucalyptus tree are supplementary activities undertaken by model farmers in larger scales. Both have use and market values, as the *gesho* is needed for the production of *tella* and *tej* (both home brewed traditional alcoholic drinks) and is sold in the market usually for the production of *araki* (traditional distilled liquor), which is a widespread activity in the nearby *woreda* of Dembecha. The same is true of eucalyptus because its seed pods, leaves, branches and wood are used for household firewood and sold for the same purpose. Moreover, the limbs and log of eucalyptus trees are not only important construction materials but also sold for collectors and individual users.

As quite a few model farmers have stated, it is noteworthy here that these and other supplementary activities have backward linkages in making more money through the sale of seedlings of eucalyptus and grafted fruit trees (for prices of 2-10 birr per seedling) to other farmers in their localities. Similarly, the sale of animal feed harvested on plots that are less productive for crop farming has brought significant incomes for model farmers engaged in the venture.

Last but not least in the current category of supplementary activities are poultry and apiculture. Many of the interviewed model farmers, particularly in Ziyew Shiwun, stated that they have started to engage in modern poultry using day-old chicken supplied to them from the *woreda* office of agriculture and rural development. They noted that, given the significant increase in the price of chicken, they have benefited from this venture. However, they pointed out that lack of sustainable supply of feed and chicken diseases as problems that reduced the profitability of the activity. Regarding apiculture, the local demands of honey for making *tej* as well as regional and national demands make the activity profitable. In recognition of these advantages, many model farmers have started modern apiculture or modernized their traditional setups. Again, the price and supply of modern bee hives and the ecological unsuitability of some locations in the study areas were raised as challenges. It is noteworthy here that despite the challenges the income derived from such activities is high enough to warrant the continued engagement of farmers in the activities and their scaling up.

5.1.4 Non-agricultural Business Ventures

As their financial capacity increases, model farmers commonly venture into non-agricultural businesses. The most common of such ventures is the construction of houses in small market towns of the *woreda* (like Kuch), roadside towns (such as Mankusa), Bure town and even in the regional capital Bahir Dar. These houses are often rented to students and government employees as residential quarters. In addition, some model farmers rent these houses to serve as restaurants, stores and shops.[22] In some cases, successful model farmers set up flour mills in the rural *kebeles* as well as market towns.

Plate 4: A Mule-Drawn Cart Owned by a Model Farmer in Ziyew Shiwun *Kebele* (Left) and a House Constructed and Rented by a Female Model Farmer in Fetam Sentom (Right)

---

[22] A few model farmers who built houses in towns use them for the residence of part of the family, for example, school-going children. These houses are sometimes fully furnished and likely to accommodate the whole family in the near future.

Plate 5: A Grain Store in Kuch Town Owned by a Model Farmer in Ziyew Shiwun *Kebele*

It was also found that model farmers buy mule drawn carts for own use as well as to rent for other farmers. The market value of such carts is particularly high both in the rural *kebele* and small towns of the study areas; and they bring in extra income to farmers. In the rural villages, they are used to transport compost, fertilizers, seeds and harvest between different places. In the market towns, they serve as means of transportation of cereals between the market place, grain stores and flour mills.

Carrying out wholesale grain trade is the fourth off-farm business venture undertaken by interviewed model farmers.[23] Even though the activity is undertaken by only a few exceptionally successful model farmers, many more farmers may engage in this activity in the future.

5.2   Contribution to Poverty Reduction

If Ethiopia's poverty reduction strategy is to be successful, the needs of the farmers must be addressed. As far as rural household needs are concerned, ensuring food security is at the fore-front. The success of peasant entrepreneurs must be first and foremost gauged by its impact on the alleviation of poverty at the rural household level. This is also a key goal in the country's drive towards food self-sufficiency and in reducing poverty. In this regard, four areas of improvement, which are experienced by model farmers are discussed below.

---

[23] Even though only two of the model farmers interviewed had grain stores and were engaged in the wholesale business, interviewed community members also pointed out the existence of other model farmers who own grain stores in nearby towns, such as Kuch in Ziyew Shiwun and Fetam in Fetam Sentom.

- *Household food security*

The prevalence of household food insecurity in rural areas is one of the key manifestations of poverty. Hence, tackling rural poverty requires ensuring food security – that is freedom from hunger and starvation. In this regard, all model farmers interviewed in this study indicated that they have successfully met their food security needs – that is, they are now able to feed their families throughout the year. They live in houses made of corrugated iron sheet,[24]with partitions for a living room, a bedroom and space for animals. Some of them have furnished their houses with modern household appliances like a sofa, a dinning table and a TV set (see Plate 6).

Apart from adequately feeding family members, being able to prepare *tella* at home and entertain themselves throughout the dry as well as the rainy seasons is a good indicator of food security. Model as well as non-model farmers interviewed agreed that most model farmers belong to this category of rural households, who are not constrained by shortage of crops to prepare the widely consumed local drink *(tella)* throughout the year.

Model farmers have done so by increasing the volume of farm production from year to year, by diversifying their farm activities (i.e. by growing different crops during a given production season) and by undertaking non-farm activities. As has been discussed, model farmers have been increasing farm production mainly in two ways. Firstly, they have been able to increase production by expanding size of cultivated plots through renting land. Renting additional plot puts extra pressure on farmers to increase production and be profitable. Otherwise, it would be difficult to cover the cost of rentals. Being profitable, in turn enhances their ability to access land for rent as productive farmers are often sought by those who give their land for rent.

Secondly, farm production has been increasing through on-farm diversification – that is, producing different types of crops. By looking at the profile of interviewed model farmers, it is easy to note that the average model farmer cultivates more crop varieties than non-model farmers. It is not only the variety and quantity of crops produced but also the orientation of model farmers to produce high value crops that make them successful rural entrepreneurs. Integrating production of cash crops (e.g. red pepper, fruits, etc.) into the small farm business has the advantage of helping farm households conserve staple crops from being sold at depressing prices (especially immediately after the harvest season) to meet various obligations, such as paying land tithe, school

---

[24]Although most farmers in the study area have built houses covered with CIS, model farmers' houses have better quality in terms of internal partitioning, quality of construction materials, number of CIS used, etc.

fees for children and health care expenses. At present, cash-oriented model farmers can cover such expenses from the sale of cash crops so that crops produced for consumption (e.g. wheat, maize) can last longer.

Thirdly, model farmers have managed to increase household income by undertaking non-farm activities. For example, operating a horse-drawn cart, running tea/coffee shops and building a house in a nearby town to be rented and many other sideline income generating activities are intended to strengthen the financial capacity of model farmers. Most of the model farmers interviewed are engaged in one or more of these income generating activities. Some have even surpassed the objective of meeting household food security and started accumulating assets in the form of cash savings, shares in cooperatives, and building houses in towns. This may be stating the obvious but households with diversified income sources (as exhibited by model farmers) are less likely to be vulnerable to food insecurity and hence to poverty than those that depend exclusively on crop production as the only means of livelihood. Increasing food production and raising income at the household level contributes to the reduction of poverty among farmers. a

- *Education of children*

Education is one of the anti-poverty millennium development goals and is seen by parents as the only means to escape rural poverty. Rural parents are now convinced that they are no longer in a position to divide their plots to their (male) children when the latter become adults. As a result, they are determined to educate their children as a way of building their future. They try to invest whatever limited resources they have to provide education for their children.

This is especially true of model farmers who are expected to set an example for other farmers by sending their children to school. The interviewed model farmers indicated that they are now able to send their children to school and can provide educational materials and school uniforms. Some even have managed to send their children to private colleges in Bure, Finote Selam, Debre Markos and even Bahir Dar by covering all expenses including transportation and accommodation costs and school fees.

- *Access to health services*

Increased crop production and income has enabled model farmers and their families to access better health services. They can now afford money to pay for health services and drugs not only in government health institutions but also in private health centers that charge relatively higher prices. There is another dimension by which model farmers have become health-conscious. In this instance, worth citing is the active participation of model farmers in the government health extension program, which has helped them to take practical steps to minimize health-related risks. Preparing separate containers for storing water for drinking and cooking, efforts to dispose waste responsibly and separating human habitation from animals are some of the important health-safeguards that are undertaken by model farmers.

- *Access to credit*

One of the manifestations of rural poverty is that resource-poor farmers do not have access to credit. However, model farmers, because of their good discipline in the management of loans, have established good reputation with local and regional micro-finance institutions. For example, the Bure *Woreda* ACSI branch office has identified model farmers as less risky borrowers that do not default loans. Hence, the ACSI is often more willing to extend loans to model farmers than to non-model farmers.

It needs to be pointed out that some model farmers have credit needs which could not be met by the local financial institutions such as ACSI (see 5.2 for details). To cope with the problem, some model farmers have developed their financial capacity by regularly saving money in local credit and saving cooperatives. This is, for example, true of a 33-year-old model farmer in Ziyew Shiwun, who is a member of the Genet Ber Credit and Savings Cooperative. This farmer and his wife were saving monthly 20 and 10 Birr respectively. In this way, the household has broadened its access to credit and financial resources and this in turn has enabled them to access extension inputs thereby increasing farm production and tackling poverty.

- *Community-level poverty alleviation ventures*

The success of model farmers goes beyond personal and family benefits, to the neighborhood and community levels. Model farmers not only inspire but also give advice to the non-model farmers on how to improve their on and off farm ventures. In fact, some non-model farmers admitted that they benefited from the advice they received from model farmers and from their successes. For example, non-model farmers whose plots share boundaries with model farmers stated in explicit terms that they have changed their fertilizer application methods by observing the practice of model farmers. In the past, these farmers were not applying the right amount of chemical fertilizers on the right time. Because of this their yields were poor. Learning from the experiences of model farmers, they have now started to apply fertilizers as recommended by DAs (see also section 6.2).

Some successful model farmers have become investors in the agricultural sector by undertaking small scale commercial agriculture and providing employment for members of the community in which they work. This has created employment opportunities mostly for landless young people who are employed as full-time farm laborers and daily laborers who work on model farmers' plots during the peak agricultural seasons. This is especially true of model farmers in Fetam Sentom and to some extent in Ziyew Shiwun, where rental land is available to expand farming and the agro-ecology is favorable to grow crops for commercial purposes. Based on our observation, it will not be an exaggeration to state that a distinctive group of farmers who is convinced that farming can indeed be made profitable is in the process of emerging amongst model farmers.

Plate 6: A House Constructed by a Model Farmer in Kuch Town (Left) and House of a Model Farmer in Ziyew Shiwun *Kebele (Right)*

Plate 7: A Well-furnished Living Room of a House Constructed by a Model Farmer in Kuch Town

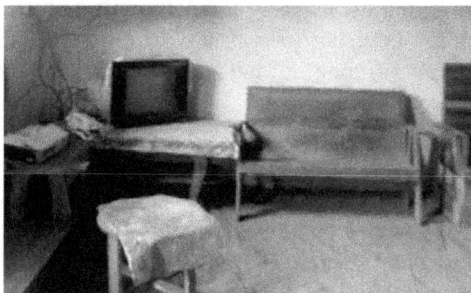

5.3   Inter-Kebele Differences

It was found that the entrepreneurial measures discussed earlier are not taken by model farmers in all of the study *kebeles* uniformly. The study has found out that inter-*kebele* differences were caused by agro-ecological factors and access to infrastructure. The differences can be summarized as follows.

•   *Weheni Durbete*

 Farmer entrepreneurship in this *kebele* is characterized by farm intensification in response to small land holding and lack of opportunities of land expansion through rent. Thus, use of chemical fertilizers, compost preparation and improved seeds to increase productivity of plots are undertaken by model farmers. Model farmers also engage in planting *gesho* and eucalyptus tree in their residential compounds and communal plots.

Another most common supplementary agricultural venture in the *kebele* is sheep fattening, which is largely motivated by the ecological suitability of the area. According to the *kebele* DA, while sheep fattening is practiced by model and non-model farmers alike, the former are more likely to engage in a more regular and organized manner (e.g. providing adequate feed for the animals). In most cases, model farmers keep on average five or more sheep for fattening while, non-model farmers commit less number of sheep for this endeavor.   This difference is owing to the fact that while most model farmers see sheep fattening as an economic opportunity that needs to be expanded, non-model farmers do not appear to pursue this endeavor as a serious business.

•   *Ziyew Shiwun*

The *kebele* has agro-ecological features suitable for crop farming. As a result, most activities of farmer entrepreneurship revolve around crop production and marketing. Generally, crop diversification and scaling up production are more commonly practiced in this *kebele* than in other study *kebeles*. Thanks to its access to road, maize seed multiplication is widely practiced in the *kebele.* For example, about 55 hectares were cultivated for the production of maize seed in the *meher* season of 2010. Owing to the same factor, grain trade is a common activity of farmer entrepreneurs in the study area. For example, in August 2010, a model farmer in Kuch, who owns a grain store, was buying crops from farmers with the intention of supplying to grain traders of Bure and Finote Selam towns. Only model farmers who can command adequate cash and own a store are able to afford this during a time of the year when most farmers are struggling to feed their family members.

- ***Fetam Sentom***

Farmer entrepreneurship in this *kebele* is characterized by activities aimed at increasing productivity and scaling up production, namely vertisol management and renting land. The *kebele* has 189 hectares of vertisol, out of which 50 hectares have been cultivated using BBM. According to the coordinator of the *kebele* rural development station, the majority of those who applied the BBM are model farmers. Moreover, using the availability of land as an opportunity, all of the interviewed farmers indicated that they increased production by renting plots from other farmers. Key informants also indicated this reality. In addition, the *Kebele* is suitable for production of cash crops such as sesame, red pepper and fruits. Many model farmers are more commonly engaged in these activities and many of those interviewed indicated that they had plans to expand such operations in the future.

5.4   Challenges and Prospects

5.4.1 Challenges

Farming is inherently full of risks and challenges. Broadly, two types of challenges can be identified here: environment/ecological and socio-economic/policy related. A brief discussion of these two is in order.

Firstly, the main environmental hazard/risk factors associated with farming are particularly uncertainty with the amount and time of rainfall. This is a constant source of concern for farmers dependent on rain-fed agriculture. Secondly, crops are vulnerable to attacks by insects, hail and frost, all of which often cause substantial damage to the farm economy. Thirdly, centuries of crop cultivation and population pressures have led to depletion of ecological resources (e.g. soil degradation and deforestation). These factors obviously limit farmers' entrepreneurial ventures. Farmers in the study areas have little control over many of the challenges mentioned above and hence are at the mercy of nature.

Now, returning to the socio-economic/policy related challenges, four issues are relevant. These are (1) lack of dependable markets for farm produce; (2) shortage of cultivable land; (3) shortage of financial capital; and (4) uncertainty in the supply of extension inputs. Regarding the first point, discussions with farmers revealed that model farmers are no longer guided in their production decisions by the instinct of producing for household consumption. While this objective is still central to the household economy, producing goods and services for the market is increasingly becoming important since model farmers also need cash to buy extension inputs.

However, most of the model farmers interviewed indicated that the price of farm produce is lagging behind the price of manufactured products. They specifically mentioned the case of fertilizer prices, which have been rising steadily while the price of *teff* has not been increasing as much as fertilizer. Interviewed farmers further noted that *teff*, which, according to them, used to be sold from birr 800 to 1000 per quintal three years back, but is now fetching Birr 500 to 600 only. Some also mentioned how soap prices have doubled in the last two years while maize prices have been unreasonably low. Most farmers attribute the problem to exploitation by the middlemen and called for government intervention to correct the unbalanced terms of trade between farm and industrial products[25].

This may be stating the obvious but it needs to be reiterated that farmer entrepreneurship is unthinkable without adequate land. Most model farmers interviewed expressed that shortage of land was their major concern. Of course, the level of scarcity of land varies among the three studied *Kebeles*. In the *dega Kebele* of Weheni Durbete, for example, land shortage is acute and hence the possibility for farm expansion through land rent is very limited. It is a community where every household tries to engage in intensive cultivation of crops on small plots of land. In the *woinadega Kebele* of Ziyew Shiwun, on the other hand, the land problem may not appear as alarming but still concern was expressed by most model farmers, who are eager to expand their farm operations. Some farmers try to mitigate the problem of shortage of land by renting land from *qolla* farmers and also by practicing inter-cropping, for example, of cereals with oilseeds.

Although some model farmers try to avoid loans from ACSI and local saving and credit cooperatives (for fear of debt), others expressed dissatisfaction with the lack of sufficient amount of credit that will enable them to expand their farm-based entrepreneurial activities. For example, a 38 year-old model farmer from Ziyew Shiwun *Kebele*, planned to undertake commercial farming in the *qolla* areas by borrowing up to 50,000 Birr. However, he could not find a lender of this loan size as ACSI has adopted a very conservative lending policy toward the farming sector setting the maximum amount of loan for rural borrowers at no more than 7000 Birr. In the eyes of highly motivated model farmers ACSI's loans are meager and do not help to expand farm activities along commercial lines. Their growing need for cash can be met only when commercial banks consider them as trustworthy borrowers like investors.

From our observation of the study area, it can be stated that farmers in general and model farmers in particular are worried about their helpless dependence on

---

[25]This only reflects market conditions at the time of data collection as prices often fluctuate between the years.

chemical fertilizers to grow even the most basic food crops, such as *teff* and wheat. Their concern is based on two basic reasons; namely (1) Ethiopia does not produce chemical fertilizers and hence heavily relies on external suppliers; and (2) dependence on the foreign fertilizer market contributes to the volatile upward moving nature of fertilizer prices. With regard to the first point, farmers fear that the external source may not be sustainable not only in terms of production but also transporting it inland because Ethiopia does not own a port. Regarding prices, farmers were quick to point out how the cost of a quintal of DAP has doubled in less than a decade. Some farmers, however, countered this observation by stating that the price of *teff* has more than tripled in the last five years alone.

5.4.2 Prospects

Although some of the challenges facing model farmers seem insurmountable (e.g. environmental/ ecological factors) most of the model farmers interviewed were optimistic about their future. What sets apart model farmers from other farmers is the strong view held by the former that farming can be rewarding and profitable if serious attention is given to it. Such farmers are convinced that investors and business leaders can emerge from the farming community if there are improvements in market access and in the provision of capital and land, and other inputs. However, it should be noted that unlike *woinadega* and *qolla* farmers, *dega* farmers are not that optimistic about their future.

Model farmers see prospects for their further development on two fronts (1) within farming; and (2) outside farming. It can be pointed out that some model farmers are keen to expand their entrepreneurial activities by focusing on farming and related activities. They have recognized opportunities for expansion by cultivating high value crops (e.g. pepper), by producing twice a year using water/rope/pedal pump irrigations or by tapping water from streams/springs. For example, one model farmer in Weheni Durbete, who is constrained by shortage of land, plans to rent land located near a river stream so that he can plant potato in the dry season. A relatively resourceful model farmer in Ziyew Shiwun, who manages 8 hectares of cultivable land (2 hectares his own and 6 hectares rented), plans to acquire additional land in the *qolla* and convert it into a commercial plantation. Another model farmer in the same *Kebele* plans to introduce mango and papaya fruits to his garden crops of *gesho* and coffee. Increased production of eucalyptus seedlings for sale, sheep fattening, introducing modern beehives and poultry farming have also been identified by one or more model farmers as potential areas for development.

Since farming alone will not satisfy the increased demand for consumption and cash (for example, to cover school expenses, pay for fertilizer, buy clothes, etc.)

it is essential to identify and tap additional income generating activities outside farming. Some farmers have seen that exclusive dependence on farming makes them vulnerable to food insecurity. Crops harvested in a given production season can last longer if they are devoted to consumption and less for the market to pay extension inputs and school expenses. Most model farmers interviewed have developed a sense of recognition of the value of diversification of income sources outside farming and there is a tendency among them to augment farm income with non-farm incomes. As was stated earlier, examples of non-farm income generating activities commonly undertaken by model farmers include operating a small marketing enterprise, building a house for rent, managing and renting horse cart and running coffee/tea shops and small restaurants.

Case 3: Aspiration of a Young Model Farmer to be an Investor

A 33 year-old farmer in Ziyew Shewun *Kebele* has started farming at the age of 15 under the guidance of his uncle. He got 0.5 ha of land through land redistribution that was carried out in 1996. Currently, he farms 5 ha of additional land through rent and applied 9 quintals of fertilizer during the 2009 *meher season* (all his purchases paid in cash) and produced 65 quintals of maize, 46 quintals of wheat, 8 quintals of chickpeas, 9 quintals of teff and 9 quintals of millet. He also planted 500 eucalyptus trees and 50 *gesho* trees around his farm. His farm activities are supported by 4 oxen, 2 cows, 6 calves and dozens of sheep and goats plus a cart mule and two donkeys. He has plans to expand his farming by renting land in the *qolla* so that he can grow such high value crops like sesame and red pepper. He has employed two people who would help him with his expanding farm activities. He said his grade 6 education has helped him record some key aspects of his farm decisions, such as fertilizer purchases, and compare expenses with amount of crops produced. He found that applying fertilizer is profitable. In the last 10 years, since he started farming independently, he has accumulated some money, which he will use it to build a warehouse in Kuch town and start grain trading business. His three school children are well-fed throughout the year and have enough clothes to wear both in and outside school. His aim is to send them to college/university and by then he is confident he will have enough money to pay school fees.

In Ziyew Shiwun, model farmers have their eyes focused on opening a small marketing business at Kuch town. Some have already done so like the 38 year old-farmer who constructed a warehouse to buy and store grains during the harvest season and then sell it when prices pick up during the *meher* season. He has also rented space to other farmers and collects income. Combining farming and trade activities represents the future aspiration of model farmers like him.

Another model farmer in Ziyew Shiwun *Kebele* is operating horse carts to transport agricultural goods in the villages during the harvest season and to transport goods and people within and to and from Kuch town. Many more model farmers are engaged in the horse cart renting business to transport people and goods within and between Kuch and surrounding villages. Quite a few model farmers have built houses, e ach partitioned into student dormitories in anticipation of the upgrading of the Kuch Secondary School into a college Preparatory School. Others plan to establish tea/coffee shops and small restaurants designed to cater for the needs of preparatory school students.

5.5 Model Farmers in the Eyes of the Community

One of the major objectives of this study was to identity whether the qualities, skills and knowledge of model farmers are being learnt and adopted by other farmers in the community. Moreover, since any adoption of these attributes by other farmers is going to depend on the way they see model farmers (whether as change agents or merely lucky or favored), it is important to consider the opinions of the former about the latter. In the sections that follow, this issue will be addressed based on FGDs with community members and interviews with key informants.

5.5.1 Community Perception towards Model Farmers

The overwhelming majority of informants in the study communities recognize model farmers for what they are – hard working and enterprising individuals who work closely with DAs and are at the forefront of technology adoption. Mentioning model farmers in their community by name, community members stressed that these farmers attained their status not as a result of ascription or a windfall but because they went ahead of their fellow farmers and engaged in activities that enabled them to produce more and better and thus earn more money. It was further added that once successful, these model farmers built on their successes to intensify and diversify agricultural production and venture into non-farm activities.

To investigate the issue in depth, informants were asked if all model farmers were deserving of the title or not. The responses were once again positive. Respondents stated that model farmers are indeed role models from whom others can learn. However, it is important here to note that a participant of a FGD in Ziyew Shiwun expressed his misgivings. He said some model farmers do not live up to the standards set for them as testified by the status of their plots, which in some cases are observed to have suffered from soil erosion. Similarly, the respondents were asked if they know farmers in their community whose achievements surpass those of model farmers, but were not recognized as such by the relevant authorities. Again, respondents stated that the best and most achieving farmers in the community were recognized as model farmers.

The FGDs further revealed that not only are model farmers looked up to for their knowledge and skill of farm and business management but also for the way they manage their household and personal behavior. Often, model farmers are stated to have a stable family where members care for each other. Moreover, they are praised for their upbringing of children and the fact that they are free from addiction to alcohol and avoidance of unnecessary expenses. In short, most model farmers are seen as exemplary in their way of life.

The study further investigated if people's perceptions of model farmers are reflected in practices, for instance, in the participation of model farmers in community affairs. It was found that model farmers are actively involved in community affairs in one way or another. Informants stated that these farmers often acted as mediators; marriage solicitors; and members of committees dealing with various affairs; community representatives; and chairmen, secretaries or treasurers of *iddirs*[26] and other community-based organizations. Moreover, a few of the model farmers are currently serving in the local administration in various capacities.

5.5.2 *Impact of Model Farmers on Other Community Members*

Poverty reduction at the community level cannot be achieved if success on and off the farm is limited to a handful of farmers and the bulk of the farming community keeps on using backward farming techniques and stays dependent on subsistence farming. In light of this fact, the study attempted to find out if non-model farmers have learnt from the best practices of model farmers and taken measures to improve their livelihoods. It was found that diffusion of knowledge and techniques of model farmers is occurring through two major channels. First, informal and person-to-person contacts. Our interviews with community members revealed that farmers learn valuable lessons which they try to apply and benefit from through their day-to-day contact with model farmers in and around the village, market place, and social gatherings.

The second channel is a more formal and institutionalized mechanism through which farmers learn from each other. This channel includes the participation of model farmers in development teams and farmer festivals. Model farmers participate in development teams that comprise 20-30 household heads who are

---

[26]Indigenous, community based voluntary association established primarily to provide mutual aid during death of family member.

beneficiaries of agricultural extension packages. The reasons for setting up these development teams are to facilitate contact of farmers with DAs, transfer technology, facilitate experience sharing among farmers and deliver extension services and farm inputs easily. These teams have 4-5 leaders, who coordinate their activities. These leaders are almost always model farmers who liaise between farmers who are members of the development team and DAs. Moreover, they are entrusted with the task of transferring new technologies and techniques they have learnt to the farmers in the development team. Community members who are organized in development teams under the leadership of model farmers state that these farmers effectively carry out their responsibilities of coordination and technology and knowledge transfer.

Benefiting even more, however, are members of development sub-teams (commonly known as 5 to 1 arrangements which constitute 4 to 6 non-model farmers organized under one model farmer who is dubbed as the supporter. Since the arrangement requires frequent follow up by the leader of the sub-team, members of the teams are often neighbors or have plots that border each other. This arrangement has an incremental effect as the members often tend to be relatives or close friends with each other, and therefore have other spheres of contact and influence in addition to the development sub-team. When asked about the benefits they gained from model farmers through the development sub-team, informants from all study *kebeles* stated that they have received follow up and hands-on training by sub-team leaders. An informant in Weheni Durbete *kebele* organized under a model farmer describes his experience as follows:

> *The things I learnt from him [*the sub-team leader, model farmer*] are many. When compost preparation was first introduced last year, he learnt quick and started using compost on his farm. Then, describing to us the benefits of using compost he urged us to start preparing it. Whenever I have difficulty in preparing compost I go to him and ask him for advice, which he willingly provides. As a result, I prepared compost and now I am using it on a plot on which I have planted maize. Same is true regarding digging a toilet. When health extension workers started teaching us about the benefit of digging a toilet, he dug one immediately and started using it. As usual, he kept on coming to the homes of the four farmers under him [including the interviewee] and telling us about the benefits of digging a toilet. Following him, we dug a toilet in our compound. Unfortunately, the toilet I dug collapsed. Yesterday, he came to my house, and when he saw that the toilet has collapsed, he admonished me for not fixing it promptly. I fixed the toilet the same evening under the light of the moon. Of the things he has done and I have found to be beneficial, I am now left with building an enclosure (separate from my house) for cattle. That, I am going to do soon.*

There are many such stories of taking lessons from model farmers. In fact, each member of the development sub-teams interviewed by the researchers had something to say in relation to the lessons they have learnt from model farmers. Model farmers who are leaders of 5 to 1 arrangements were asked if the farmers they are supposed to support and coach take and apply the lessons provided to them properly. Accordingly, most responded by saying that most of the farmers organized around them are fast learners who try their best to apply the knowledge and skill they were taught. A model farmer in Ziyew Shiwun states his experience as follows:

> *As I do not want to be the sole successful farmer in my community, I always give advice to others. There are five farmers organized around me. When I prepare compost, apply fertilizer, sow, or start weeding, I go to them and tell them that I have started doing so and urge them to follow suit. Our motto is 'let's grow together'. Even though the rate of acceptance varies from person to person, the five farmers in my team follow my steps carefully. In particular, one of them has become a better farmer after adopting techniques of proper fertilizer application from me. He himself testified to this.*

The second institutionalized mechanism through which learning from model farmers involves the use of farmer field days and inter-*kebele* tours organized by the *woreda* office for agriculture and rural development and the IPMS Bure pilot project. Under this arrangement, farmers who can serve as role models for others in crop production, livestock fattening and dairy products, horticulture, apiculture, and natural resource management are selected and their farms or production areas visited by other farmers. An informant from the *woreda* office of agriculture and rural development provides the case of a 48 year-old farmer (see Case 2) as an example of such practice. When this farmer solved the water logging problem of a plot, with vertisol type soil[27] and increased the productivity of his plot, farmers in the *kebele* were taken to his plot and shown what he achieved. That, the informant argues, has contributed significantly to the recent popularity of the BBM in that particular *kebele*.

---

[27]It has got high clay content with swelling/shrinking properties.

6. Conclusion and Recommendation

6.1 Conclusion

The purpose of this study was to investigate the various aspects of peasant entrepreneurship focusing on the experiences and achievements of model farmers. This group comprises a highly motivated section of the farming community who are serving as a catalyst for the implementation of the government extension package program. The achievements of the Ethiopian extension service in the last 15 years are measured, among other things, in terms of the number of model farmers in each *Kebele*. This is taken by all stakeholders at all levels in the delivery of the extension service as an important indicator of the success of the extension package program. In each harvest season, farmers' festivals are held starting from *Kebele* levels all the way to the regional state at Bahir Dar to celebrate the achievements of model farmers and to motivate other farmers to follow the example of successful model farmers.

This study was conducted in Bure *Woreda* of west Gojjam zone of the Amhara National Regional State. The region is part of west Amhara which, favored by relative abundance of moisture compared to east Amhara, is characterized by high utilization of extension inputs, especially chemical fertilizers. Bure *Woreda* has a long history of extension service as reflected in high-consumption of chemical fertilizers. The farmers in Bure and their plots have developed a strong association with chemical fertilizers and this association has evolved into one of 'dependency' so much that nowadays it is impossible to think of cereal cultivation without getting access to fertilizers.

Within Bure *Woreda* three *kebeles* were selected for an in-depth exploration and understanding of the situation of model farmers. The three *kebeles* representing *dega*, *woinadega* and *qolla* agro-ecology zones respectively were Weheni Durbete, Ziyew Shiwun and Fetam Sentom. The selection was done in consultation with staff of the Bure *Woreda* agriculture and rural development office. The inclusion of the three agro-ecologically different *Kebeles* in the study made it possible to compare the distribution and experiences of model farmers across the *dega-woinadega-qolla* ecology spectrum. It also created an opportunity to appreciate the impact of agro-ecological factors on the activities of model farmers.

Because of the nature of the topic under investigation the study utilized qualitative research methods of in-depth interviews, focus group discussions and field observations supplemented by secondary data collected from agriculture development station offices' of the respective study *kebeles*, Bure *Woreda* agriculture and rural development office, from Bure *Woreda* ACSI branch office, Bure *Woreda* cooperative organization and promotion office and also from such regional organizations as BOARD, ACSI, AISCO and ARARI. Observations of selected sites (e.g. maize seed multiplication plots, water pump projects, compost preparation sites) were used to generate qualitative data relevant to the study. Most of the qualitative data used in this study were collected from model farmers, non-model farmers, *Kebele* officials, DAs and to some extent from health extension workers. The data collected were analyzed using a variety of interpretive methods, such as thematic analysis, comparative method, case studies and visual descriptions using photos and tables.

Based on qualitative data gathered from the field and corroborated by secondary data, the research found out that:

1. The phenomenon of peasant entrepreneurship best epitomized by the behavior and conduct of model farmers is much more widespread among the farming population than often thought or imagined. However, it varies from community to community, mainly resulting from agro-ecological variations that dictate the type of entrepreneurial activity to be carried out and the level of success of such activities.

2. Model farmers are characterized by strong orientation to improvement and change, creativity and innovation, new ways of generating income and making profit; pro-activeness and willingness to take risk; farsightedness and forward planning.

3. In addition, model farmers exhibit one or more of the following background characteristics:

   • Many of them had worked as sharecroppers before they became independent farmers.

   • Almost all of them have attended some level of formal education, usually up to grade 6.

   • They tend to be hardworking farmers who cultivated plots that usually exceed the amount of land given to them through land redistribution carried out in 1996..

   • Most of them have some kind of external experience such as service in the *kebele* administration, serving in the army; and a few of them worked as migrant laborers.

4. Most model farmers are actively participating in the agricultural extension program and they are more likely to benefit from their participation than non-model farmers. This is attributable to their

adherence to instructions given by DAs regarding correct application technology packages.

5. In response to the obvious success of pioneering farmers and their followers, the local community has developed a positive attitude towards model farmers and has become very supportive of their entrepreneurial activities.

6. As far as their level of access to the different capital assets is concerned, some seem to have an initial advantage in certain areas, such as access to finance through support from kin/friend but not in other areas, such as initial size of landholdings, fertility of plots and access to water source, which appear to be more or less similar across the communities studied.

7. Recent initiatives, such as the health extension package and establishment and expansion of cooperatives, seem to provide more benefit to model farmers than other farmers. The former seem to be actively involved in the implementation of the above initiatives.

8. The presence of law and order in the area, which in part is a result of the active participation of model farmers themselves, seems to contribute to success of model farmers in their entrepreneurial activities.

9. Most model farmers seem to be engaged in multiple innovative farming and non-farm activities, including the following:

    - Growing different crops in different agro-ecological zones in order to minimize risk and at the same time to increase production;

    - Diversification into high value market crops such as sesame, red pepper, fruits (e.g. papaya) and vegetables (e.g. onion) and spices (e.g. *tikur azmud*[28]);

    - Extending diversification into supplementary income generating activities, such as cattle fattening, sheep fattening, apiculture, poultry, production of seedlings (e.g. eucalyptus) and growing eucalyptus and *gesho* as cash crops;

    - Undertaking non-agricultural activities, such as construction of houses for commercial purposes, running grain stores in small towns, running small businesses (e.g. eateries), establishing flour mills and running horse carts.

---

[28] *Foeniculum vulgare*, seed of the Fennel herb used as spice.

10. Most model farmers are seen by their communities as role models to be emulated. This has helped them and DAs to positively influence other fellow farmers and to mobilize the community for positive change.

6.2 Recommendations

In light of the empirical evidence documented in this study, the following recommendations are forwarded:

1. The contribution of formal education to farmer entrepreneurship has been noted by this study. Therefore, there is a need to continue the progress made so far in making primary education accessible to all, including through expanding adult education.

2. Model farmers have benefited from external experience acquired through migration. Obviously, not all farmers can migrate. Therefore, information on best practices should be available to farmers through mass media channels such as radio, TV, and printed materials. Such information can cover a wide range of issues, including market information.

3. Training related to various technology packages is important for the success of farmer entrepreneurs. In connection to this, FTCs are best situated to serve the needs of farmers through regular training. For this, DAs have to be adequately trained, well-remunerated and provided with facilities in order for them to carry out their tasks effectively. Support should be given to under-equipped FTCs in the form of teaching aids and office equipment. Moreover, in order to promote farmer entrepreneurship, FTCs should provide business development-oriented training targeted at entrepreneurial farmers.

4. While the attention given to model farmers by DAs is important so that model farmers will not slide back from their current status, similar attention should be given to the rest of the farming community so that potentially entrepreneurial farmers can be brought up to the level that is reached by model farmers now. In addition to the activities of DAs, the current 5 to 1 approach of organizing village level development sub-teams for the purpose of strengthening farmers' entrepreneurial activities should be strengthened.

5. Cooperatives of various types were found to be supportive of farmer entrepreneurship. This is particularly true of saving and credit cooperatives, which are making valuable contributions to the success of emerging farmer entrepreneurs. However, the lending capacity of the local saving and credit institutions should be enhanced so that they can

meet the growing credit requirements of successful peasant entrepreneurs. Alternatively, banks should be encouraged to provide loans to successful peasant entrepreneurs whose credit needs cannot be met by local saving and credit institutions.

6. As production increases, access to markets to sell agriculture produce becomes important. It is vital that farmers receive fair prices for their products and pay competitive prices for industrial goods which they buy from the market. This can be partly addressed by making market information available to farmers, like displaying prices of agricultural commodities at selected locations (a good example is an ongoing effort by Ethiopian Commodity Exchange (ECX) to display daily prices of certain agricultural commodities in Bure town). Farmers need also to be encouraged to establish consumers' cooperatives so that they can directly buy industrial products from wholesalers at fair prices.

7. The study has found that one common way of increasing production is through land renting. Therefore, the current trend towards a more secure landholding system through land registration and certification program by the regional government that permits voluntary land renting should be strengthened.

8. The study has noted the influence of agro-ecology on the activities of peasant entrepreneurs. Therefore, government policies and programs designed to encourage peasant entrepreneurship should take into account agro-ecological differences.

9. Finally, we have observed that some small towns (such as Kuch town) have begun to serve as commercial centers where model farmers are active players in the local economy. It is thus important to recognize their role and provide active support to such rural towns in the form of improving road and communications infrastructure and services so that they can grow into rural business-hubs by linking producers and consumers.

7. References

ANRS (Amhara National Regional State) Council. 2007. Regulation No. 51/2007. *Zikre-Hig Gazette.* Year 12, No. 14. 11th May. Bahir Dar.

Berhanu Gebremedhin, D. Hoekstra and Azage Tegegne. 2006. "Commercialization of Ethiopian Agriculture: Extension service from input supplier to knowledge broker and facilitator."

IPMS (Improving Productivity and Market Success) of Ethiopian Farmers Project. Working Paper 1. ILRI (International Livestock Research Institute), Nairobi, Kenya.

Bure Pilot Learning *Woreda* Diagnosis and Program Design. 2007. Bure *Woreda* Office of Agriculture and Rural Development. Bure.

Chambers, R. (1983). *Rural Development: Putting the Last First.* Harlow: Pearson Education Limited.

Cohen, J. M. (1987). Integrated Rural Development: The Ethiopian Experience and the Debate. The Scandinavian Institute of African Studies. Uppsala.

Dessalegn Rahmato (2009). "Ethiopia: Agricultural Policy Review'. Taye Assefa (ed.). Digest of Ethiopia's National Policies, Strategies and Programs. Forum on Social Studies.

_____ (2008). *The Peasant and the State: Studies in Agrarian Change in Ethiopia 1950s-2000s.* Addis Ababa: Addis Ababa University Press.

Fasil G. Kiros (1993). "The Subsistence Crisis in Africa: The Case of Ethiopia. Root Causes and Challenges of the 1990s and the New Century". Addis Ababa: Organization of Social Science Research in East Africa

Gizachew Kebede (2008) Agricultural Extension and Its Impact on Food Crop Diversity and the Livelihood of Farmers in Guduru, Eastern Wollega, Ethiopia. Norwegian University of life sciences, Norway. (MA Thesis)

Kassa Belay (2003). "Agricultural Extension in Ethiopia: The Case of Participatory Demonstration and Training Extension System." *Journal of Social Development in Africa.* Vol. 18 No 1.

Kibwana, O. T., Mitiku Haile, Laurens van Veldhuizen and Ann Waters-Bayer (2001). "Clapping with Two hands: Bringing together local and outside Knowledge for Innovation in Land Husbandry in Tanzania and Ethiopia – A Comparative Case study." *Journal of Agricultural Education.* Vol. 7, No. 3.

Mamusha Lemma and Volker Hoffmann (2005) The Agricultural Knowledge System in Tigray, Ethiopia: Empirical Study about its Recent History and Actual Effectiveness. In: Tielkes, E. et al. (Eds.), The Global Food & Product Chain – Dynamics, Innovations, Conflicts and strategies: International research on food security, natural resource management and rural development; Book of Abstracts/Tropentag 2005, October 11-13, 2005, University of Hohenheim, Stuttgart.

MoARD (Ministry of Agriculture and Rural Development). 2010. Ethiopia's Agricultural Sector Policy and Investment Framework (PIF) 2010-2020. Draft Final Report.

MoFED (Ministry of Finance and Economic Development). 2006. Plan for Accelerated and Sustained Development to End Poverty (PASDEP) (2005/06-2009/10). Addis Ababa

_____.2003. Rural Development Policy and Strategies. Economic Policy and Planning Department. Addis Ababa.

Richards, P. (1985). *Indigenous Agricultural Revolution: Ecology and Food Production in West Africa*. Hutchinson, London; Westview Press.

Rogers, EM (1983). Diffusion of Innovations. New York: Free Press.

Scoones, I. and J. Thomson (eds.). 1994. *Beyond Farmers First: Rural Peoples Knowledge, Agricultural Research and Extension Practice. Intermediate Technology Publications*. London: International Institute for Environment and Development. (which section of the book you referred if this book is a collection of articles)

Smith, L. William, Schallenkamp, K. Eichholz, and E. Douglas. 2007. "Entrepreneurial Skills Assessment: An Exploratory Study." *International Journal of Management and Enterprise Development.* Vol. 4, No.2 pp. 179 – 201.

Tesfai Tecle (1977). "An Approach to Rural Development: A Case study of the Ethiopian Package Projects." In Fasil G. Kiros (ed). *Introduction to Rural Development: A Book of Readings*. Addis Ababa: Institute of Development Research/Addis Ababa University

Wu, Bin. 2003. "Household Innovative Capacity in Marginal Areas of China: An Empirical Study in North Shaanxi." *The Journal of Agricultural Education and Extension.* Vol. 9 No 4 pp. 137 -150.

8. Annexes

Annex I: Selection Criteria for 'A', 'B' and 'C' Level Farmers

Criteria to be fulfilled by "A" Level farmers

An "A" level farmer is someone who adopts new technologies and techniques, and has improved or is improving his family's living standard. He/she is someone who:

- Uses farm inputs as per direction given [by DAs];
- Adopts new technologies quickly and applies them, and also encourages others to use the same;
- Takes care of his plots by carrying out water and soil protection measures;
- Plants trees and fruit seedlings to take care of the environment;
- Understands that time is money and thus properly uses family labor;
- Produces and uses at least $20m^3$ of compost every year;
- Helps solve problems of good governance in the *kebele/got,* and is free from such problems;
- Has changed/is changing his life by implementing health packages;
- Accepts and implements advice of experts;
- Is eager to increase his income and thus is producing/has produced market oriented products;
- Participates in meetings and is ready to share his experience with others and also share from the experiences of others;
- Has good experience in animal husbandry and fattening;
- Produces and feeds his animals improved animal feed;
- Sends school-aged children to school; and
- Is respected by community members and is willing to teach others.

Criteria to be fulfilled by "B" Level farmers

A "B" level farmer is someone who partially adopts new technologies and techniques, and is improving his family's living standard. He/she has to be someone who:

- Partially adopts new technologies;
- Partially accepts advise given by experts;

- Living standard is next to that of 'A' level farmers;
- Participates in meetings and is ready to accept and implement beneficial experiences of others;
- Can join 'A' level farmers with some supports;
- Is partially taking care of his farm;
- Produces and uses less than $20m^3$ of compost;
- Has started planting forest and fruit tree seedlings;
- Hasn't implemented all health packages Can this be checked out?; and
- Supports the solution of good governance related problems.

Criteria to be fulfilled by "C" Level farmers

A "C" level farmer is someone who was unable to improve his family's living standard by adopting new technologies and techniques despite having land and labor. He/she is someone who:

- Has not accepted new technologies and techniques so far, and is still using traditional methods of production;
- Does not accept and implement expert advice;
- Is lazy, spends his time on unproductive engagements;
- Criticizes farmers who are improving, thinks that such farmers are merely lucky rather than hardworking, and believes that wealth comes with luck;
- Does not go to meetings, criticizes those who go to meetings;
- Does not take care of his land;
- Does not send school-aged children to school;
- Does not implement health packages;
- Creates problems of good governance in the *kebele/gote;*
- Wastes household labour; and
- Does not produce and use compost.

Annex II: Criteria used in the selection of awardees

1.1   Farmers and semi-farmers

1.1.1   Farmer awardees undertaking value-added production

1. Increased exiting capital by carrying out value –added production by employing their capital in the areas of agro-processing industries, construction and trade (15)

2. Accumulated capital worth Birr 500,000 or more (20)

    a.   From capital Birr 501-999,000 ----------------------- (10)
    b.   From capital 1 million to 1.5 million ----------------- (15)
    c.   More than 1.5 million capital ------------------------- (20)

3. Guided by the market in their production and also produced for domestic and international markets (10)

4. Increased their income by growing and selling seedlings in the *Kebele* (5)

5. Persuade other farmers to become development heroes/heroines (15)

    a)   Persuaded less than 20% of the surrounding farmers (5)
    b)   Persuaded 21-30% of the surrounding farmers (7)
    c)   Persuaded 31-49% of the surrounding farmers (10)
    d)   Persuaded 50% and above of the surrounding farmers

6. Created job opportunities for the unemployed (15%)

    a) Created jobs for 5 or less people (2)
    b) Created jobs for 6-10 people (5)
    c) Created jobs for 11-19 people (10)
    d) Created jobs for 20 or more people (15)

7. Ready for and at the forefront of change and using various new technologies (10)

8. Covered their degraded land with forests and increased their incomes by undertaking agro-forestry activities on their land (5)

9. Protected their land and soils by undertaking water and soil conservation activities (5)

81

1.1.2 Farmers who have won prizes in the past and those who are semi-pastoralists

1. Achieved better results by using agricultural inputs, farming technologies, and extension services and hence accumulated more than 50,000 Birr capital and brought basic changes into their lives (20)

2. Improved the fertility of their land and worked day and night to increase productivity of their land and output (10)

   a) Increased farm productivity by 10% in 2007/08 (3)

   b) Increased farm productivity by 15% in 2007/08 (6)

   c) Increased farm productivity by 20% in 2007/08 (10)

3. Increased income by developing natural resources, forestry, producing seedlings etc. (10)

4. Able to cultivate twice a year by using ground and surface water (10)

5. Actively participate in social development works and play a leading role in the development associations (5)

6. Disassociate themselves from harmful traditional practices and strive to eradicate them (15)

7. Collect enough fodder for animals and constantly employ improved animal husbandry methods (10)

8. Covered deforested areas with trees and expanded agro-forestry techniques to increase their income (10)

9. Employed different water and soil conservation methods to conserve and protect the soils on their own land (5)

10. Protected forest on one's own area (5)

1.1.3. For youth awardees (70%)

1. Employed modern techniques on own farm and increased the productivity of their land and benefited from that (10)

2. Collected enough fodder for their animals using modern animal husbandry techniques(10)

3. Increased farm productivity using family land and benefited from it (10)

4. Converted hills and steep areas into productive farms and benefited from that and served as models for others(10)

5. Engaged in diversified activities on the side of farming and increased their income and served as models for others(10)

6. Adapted and used new technologies (10)

7. Strove to improve their lives (10)

1.1.4 For women awardees (40%)

1. Generated more than 25,000 Birr capital and beneficiated from that (10)

2. Used inputs like modern technologies and increased farm productivity with constant cultivation (10)

3. Able to help their families and send their children to school (10)

a) All school-age children attending school (10)

b) Half of all school age children attending school (5)

c) Only one child of the school-age children attending school (2)

4. Freed themselves from harmful traditional practices and backward thoughts and became an example for their peers and educate others (10)

Annex III: Profile of Interviewed Model and Non-Model Framers

Case	Kebele	Agro-ecology	Age	Sex	Educational Status	Household Size	Size of Land Holding (Ha)	Size of Rented Land (Ha)	Number of Oxen	Other business/property
					Model Farmers					
1.	Fetam	Qolla	42	Male	5	8	3	8	6	1 house for rent
2.	Fetam	Qolla	43	Male	6	5	1	17.5	4	**
3.	Fetam	Qolla	35	Female	Illiterate		3	15.625	8	1 house for rent
4.	Fetam	Qolla	50	Male	Read and Write	9	3	2.75	7	
5.	Fetam	Qolla	38	Male	9	6	2	7.25	7	1 house for rent, 1 grain store
6.	Weheni	Dega	53	Male	Read and Write	8	1	0	2	
7.	Weheni	Dega	45	Male	4	9	1.5	0.25	2	
8.	Weheni	Dega	42	Male	9	7	1	0.6675	2	
9.	Weheni	Dega	58	Male	Read and Write	8	1	1.75	4	2 mills, 2 houses for rent
10.	Weheni	Dega	50	Female	Illiterate	8	1	0	2	
11.	Weheni	Dega	34	Male	7	7	1.25	0	2	
12.	Ziyew	Woinadega	33	Male	Read and Write	6	0.5	5.25	4	Mule drawn cart
13.	Ziyew	Woinadega	53	Male	3	7	2	9	12	1 house for rent, 1 grain store
14.	Ziyew	Woinadega	46	Male	Read and Write	8	1.5	2.75	7	1 grain store, 3 houses, 3 shops
15.	Ziyew	Woinadega	38	Male	7	7	3	1	0	1 house for rent
16.	Ziyew	Woinadega	38	Male	7	7	3	1	3	1 house for rent

Abeje Berhanu and Ezana Amdework

						Non-Model Farmers				
Case	Kebele	Agro-ecology	Age	Sex	Educational Status	Household Size	Size of Land Holding (Ha)	Size of Rented Land	Number of Oxen	Other business/property
1.	Weheni	Dega	32	Male	6	4	1	0	2	-
2.	Weheni	Dega	58	Male	Illiterate	5	0.75	0	1	-
3.	Weheni	Dega	42	Male	6	6	0.5	0.25	**	-
4.	Fetam	Qolla	38	Male	Read and Write	5	1.5	2	2	-
5.	Fetam	Qolla	48	Male	Illiterate	10	1.75	2	3	-
6.	Fetam	Qolla	60	Male	6	4	3	1	2	-
7.	Ziyew	Woinadega	44	Male	6	8	4.75	0.5	5	-
8.	Ziyew	Woinadega	50	Male	Illiterate	4	3	0	4	-
9.	Ziyew	Woinadega	42	Male	Read and Write	6	1.75	0.5	**	-

Annex IV: Size of Land Cultivated and Corresponding Output of Major Crops in 2010 Meher

Model Farmers

Case	Kebele	Cereals		Pulses		Oilseeds		Pepper		Vegetables	
		Cultivated Land (Ha)	Output (Qu)	Cultivated Land (Ha)	Output (Qu)	Cultivated Land (Ha)	Output (Qu)	Cultivated Land (Ha)	Output (Qu)	Cultivated Land (Ha)	Output (Qu)
1.	Fetam	7	330	1	23	3	14	0	0	0	0
2.	Fetam	15.5	427	0	0	1	10	2	12	0	0
3.	Fetam	11	530	2.75	21	2.5	28	2	50	0.375	37
4.	Fetam	3.75	180	0.75	16	0.25	1.25	0.75	8	0	0
5.	Fetam	7.75	253	1	18	0	0	0.5	7	0.5	2
6.	Weheni	0.875	23.5	0.125	1	0	0	0	0	0	0
7.	Weheni	1.5	44	0.25	4	0	0	0	0	0	0
8.	Weheni	1.2925	40.5	0.125	2	0	0	0	0	0.25	6
9.	Weheni	2.25	70	0.25	3	0	0	0	0	0.25	30
10.	Weheni	1	27	0	0	0	0	0	0	0	0
11.	Weheni	0.75	34	0.5	1	0	0	0	0	0	0
12.	Ziyew	4.75	128	0.5	21	0	0	0.5	8	0.5	2.8
13.	Ziyew	4	256	1	15	0	0	0.75	8	0.75	0.5
14.	Ziyew	3	102	0.5	14	0	0	0.5	6	1	3
15.	Ziyew	3.5	172	0.5	3	0	0	0.5	8	0	0
16.	Ziyew	2.5	172	0.25	3	0	0	0.5	7	0	0

www.ingramcontent.com/pod-product-compliance
Lightning Source LLC
Chambersburg PA
CBHW031139270326
41929CB00011B/1684